HOUSING WITH CA

HOUSING WITH CARE

SUPPORTED HOUSING AND HOUSING ASSOCIATIONS

Lynn Watson and Rob Cooper

JR

JOSEPH
ROWNTREE
FOUNDATION

Published by
Joseph Rowntree Foundation
The Homestead
40 Water End
York YO3 6LP

Tel: (0904) 629241

ISBN 1 872470 60 2

Design by Peter Adkins Design

Printed in Great Britain by Maxiprint, York

CONTENTS

INTRODUCTION   1

CHAPTER 1: SCHEME CHARACTERISTICS AND TRENDS   11

CHAPTER 2: INFLUENCES ON SUPPORTED HOUSING   43

CHAPTER 3: FUTURE PROSPECTS   52

CHAPTER 4: POLICY CONCLUSIONS   67

APPENDICES
1 Housing Corporation definition of special needs   73
2 Comparison between the four study areas   75
3 Housing Corporation capital funding 1988 - 1992   80
4 Housing associations in the study   83

REFERENCES   84

ACKNOWLEDGEMENTS

We are very grateful for the assistance given by all those we interviewed during the course of the study. Thanks are due to the housing association staff, scheme managers, tenants and representatives of local statutory agencies and government departments who took part. Also to officers of the Housing Corporation at regional and national level and to policy and research staff at the National Federation of Housing Associations.

We wish to express thanks to the Joseph Rowntree Foundation for its support and in particular to Barbara Ballard of the Foundation for her keen interest and valuable assistance. Also to members of the research Advisory Group who offered guidance throughout the two years of the study: Rosalind Brooke, Maurice Harker, Mary Lang, Jo Lucas, Colin Mitchell, Randall Smith and Clare Ungerson. Finally, we express thanks to our friends and colleagues at Southampton University, especially Tony Rees, Graham Allan, Linda Davis, Joan Higgins and Sue High.

Lynn Watson
Rob Cooper
Department of Sociology and Social Policy
University of Southampton

INTRODUCTION

The provision of housing for people requiring extra support or care services has increased dramatically since the mid-1970s. Housing associations have played a central role in this expansion. Housing for 'special needs', with its connotations of individually tailored and small-scale provision, has been closely identified with the voluntary housing movement. Associations have been given specific encouragement to develop accommodation for special needs groups and to work in partnership with voluntary agencies and health and social services authorities. There are now over 50,000 places in supported housing schemes developed by associations in England.[1]

The idea for this study came from our experience of setting up and managing supported housing schemes in the late 1980s. It was provoked by three questions:

are housing associations providing the right kinds of housing with support?

what influences us to develop particular types of scheme?

what is the future for 'special needs', given the changing role of housing associations and their new system of funding?

The broad aims of the study are therefore to find out how the provision of supported housing has evolved to date, to pick out current trends in the development of new schemes and to identify the key influencing factors in the changing profile of the sector. The study is designed to draw conclusions relating to the types of supported housing needed in the 1990s and the capacity of housing associations and their partner agencies to develop and sustain such provision. It is intended by this means to provoke debate about future policy and practice.

Background to the study

It was the 1974 Housing Act which gave the Housing Corporation broad powers to register housing associations, to monitor their activities and to provide substantial public subsidy for the development of rented housing and hostels. The number of homes financed by the government through the Housing Corporation leaped from an average of 4,500 in the previous nine years to 37,000 in 1974. The twin principles of the new regime were fair rents and the allocation of housing according to need. This meant big changes for the Corporation, which since its inception in 1964 had 'made a modest contribution to the housing needs largely of the indigent middle classes'.[2]

Following the 1974 Housing Act, the promotion of housing for special needs groups seemed to go hand in hand with the perception of housing associations as providing a 'useful supplementary resource' to local authority housing departments.[3] The expansion of housing association activity was not intended to challenge the dominance of local authorities as housing providers and builders of new rented housing. Associations were seen rather to bring 'experience of catering for particular categories of need, such as elderly or handicapped people'.[4]

This study focuses on housing association provision which caters for groups defined by the Housing Corporation as having 'special needs'. The Corporation's definition of special needs housing has changed markedly since the mid-1970s. Special needs groups were then described as 'people who find it very difficult or impossible to find suitable privately rented accommodation, cannot afford to buy and are not eligible for a local authority house'.[5] These groups included 'the homeless, the elderly, the handicapped, singles, single parents, essential workers, ex-servicemen/women and those in tied accommodation'.[6] Today's definition is much more specific. Special needs provision is now seen as 'housing which caters for tenants with a need for a more supportive and intensive style of housing management than is found in "ordinary" housing'.[7] 'Special needs' are thus viewed as the cause rather than the consequence of people's housing difficulties. It is their support needs rather than their housing circumstances which bring them into the special needs category.

Supported housing is special needs housing by another name. The use of the terms 'supported housing' or 'housing with care and support' is growing, both because they are not value-laden and because extra support to tenants is the only feature common to all the housing schemes concerned. The ambiguity of 'special needs' can mean that the groups involved find themselves either at the top or the bottom of the list of priorities, depending on political circumstances. The term is also patronising in that it implies importance while emphasising difference. The description 'special needs' is however still widely used and it is the term usually employed by the Housing Corporation in its guidelines and policy documents. We shall refer to both special needs housing and supported housing in this report.

Supported housing schemes are expected both to cater for one of the recognised 'special needs' groups and to demonstrate a requirement for extra housing management. In listing special needs groups, the Housing Corporation recognises that the category of 'special needs' cannot be rigidly defined and circumscribed (see Appendix 1). There are tenants in mainstream housing who receive extra support but who are not included on the special needs list. Equally, there are those who may belong to one of the groups on the list but who require no additional housing management services or support.

The Housing Corporation does not prescribe particular forms of accommodation, but it will only offer capital finance through Housing Association Grant (HAG) for schemes which have the 'primary purpose' of providing housing. Certain types of schemes are specifically excluded from Corporation funding. Among these are schemes which have as their main purpose the provision of care rather than housing (for example, nursing homes), schemes which fulfil a statutory duty other than under housing legislation (for example, bail hostels) and facilities, such as respite care homes, for people who already have a permanent place to live.

The expansion of supported housing

The growth of the supported housing sector has been well-documented by the National Federation of Housing Associations, at least in respect of shared housing. Its 1990 survey of shared accommodation gives a total estimated figure of 54,071 places in 4,263 schemes in England.[8] The NFHA survey includes some unsupported schemes (for example, for students) and excludes self-contained supported housing. It cannot therefore provide a direct comparison for the present study, which looks at both shared and self-contained housing and includes only those schemes where extra support or care is offered to tenants.

The Housing Corporation produces two sets of figures relating to special needs housing. The annual summary of housing association statistics (HAR/10) gives the number of 'hostel' places provided, the term hostel being used to include all shared housing with 'warden' support. These figures indicate an increase of 13,000 places in shared special needs schemes between 1985 and 1989.[9] This represents an average increase of 8 per cent per year, as compared to an increase of between 2 per cent and 5 per cent for housing association homes in general. Figure 1 shows the location of hostel bedspaces in England and Figure 2 the regional distribution of both hostel and general housing stock.

Figure 1: Location of hostel bedspaces owned: England 1990

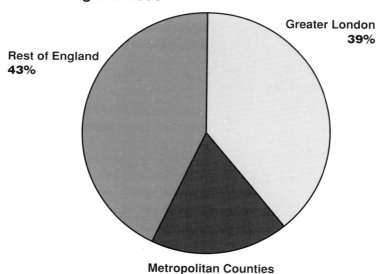

Greater London
39%

Rest of England
43%

Metropolitan Counties
18%

Total hostel bedspaces
50,200

Source: Housing Corporation, 1991, HAR/10 statistics

Figure 2: Regional distribution of housing and hostel stock

6
East Midlands
Total housing units: 47,700
% of National stock: 8%
Total bedspaces: 4,200
% of National bedspaces: 8%

1
North West
Total housing units: 66,500
% of National stock: 12%
Total bedspaces: 2,700
% of National bedspaces: 5%

7
London and Home Counties (North East and North West)
Total housing units: 119,900
% of National stock: 21%
Total bedspaces: 14,700
% of National bedspaces: 29%

2
Merseyside
Total housing units: 47,700
% of National stock: 8%
Total bedspaces: 1,700
% of National bedspaces: 3%

8
London and Home Counties (South)
Total housing units: 92,600
% of National stock: 16%
Total bedspaces: 10,500
% of National bedspaces: 21%

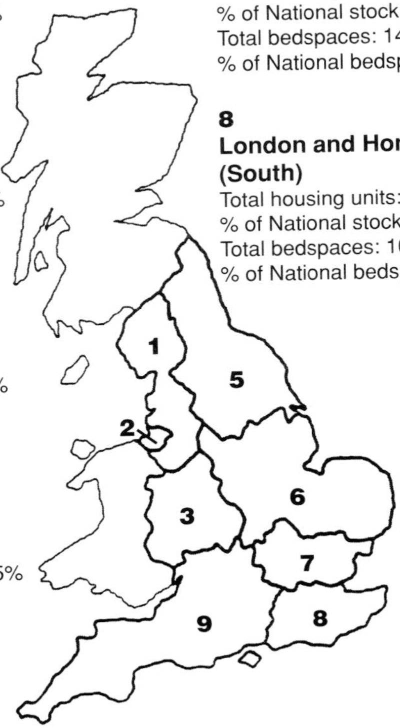

3
West Midlands
Total housing units: 54,000
% of National stock: 10%
Total bedspaces: 3,700
% of National bedspaces: 7%

4
West
Total housing units: 58,000
% of National stock: 10%
Total bedspaces: 7,400
% of National bedspaces: 15%

5
North East
Total housing units: 81,900
% of National stock: 15%
Total bedspaces: 5,300
% of National bedspaces: 11%

National totals
Housing stock: 568,300
Hostel bedspaces: 50,200

Source: Housing Corporation, 1991, HAR/10 statistics

The second set of Housing Corporation figures shows the annual allocation of capital finance to housing schemes for each of the named 'special needs' groups. These figures will include self-contained schemes as well as those offering shared accommodation. Appendix 3 gives details of recent allocations by region and group.

The changing role of housing associations

This study has been carried out against a background of major changes affecting housing associations. The Housing Corporation document 'Into the Nineties' states that associations no longer play a secondary role to local authorities. Housing associations are now seen as 'the main engine of social housing and are being funded accordingly'.[10] In fact, the ratio of investment in new housing had already shifted between 1979 and 1989 from 3:1 in favour of local authorities to 1.5:1 in favour of housing associations.[11] This change resulted from government restrictions on local authority building rather than from any substantial increase in the programme of housing associations or any priority for housing in general. In the late 1970s, housing associations were receiving annual approvals for between fifty and sixty thousand new homes. The average figure for approvals during the 1980s was around twenty-five thousand homes a year.[12] Special needs housing received between 13 per cent and 18 per cent of the annual Housing Corporation allocation in the years from 1982 to 1990.

The 1988 Housing Act introduced the requirement on housing associations to obtain a proportion of their capital for new development from private sources. At the same time, the amount of public money available through the Housing Corporation has been substantially increased. The Corporation's budget will have doubled between 1988/89 and 1992/93 (from £865.4 million to £1769.5 million). When the present study was designed, it was unclear whether special needs schemes would be expected to attract private sector loans. The eventual decision to allow 100 per cent capital subsidy from the Housing Corporation for special needs development reflected recognition that the supported housing sector could not be accommodated by the new financial regime because of its relatively high revenue costs.

During the period of the study, a new system of Housing Corporation revenue funding for special needs schemes was also introduced. The previous system of deficit funding, known as Hostel Deficit Grant (HDG), was replaced in April 1991 by Special Needs Management Allowance (SNMA). Schemes receiving HDG before that date will progressively transfer to SNMA. Key features of the new allowance are: it is a flat rate payment per 'bedspace', with lower care schemes receiving 50 per cent of the full rate; it applies to self-contained as well as shared accommodation; there must be a minimum staff:resident ratio of 1:10 for the full rate and 1:20 for the 50 per cent rate; it cannot be used for schemes with any capital funding from other (non-Housing Corporation) public sources.

Research methods

The study is concerned with housing association development in England. The four study areas were selected to give a geographical spread and a mix of London, metropolitan and non-metropolitan county areas. Two of the areas contain rural districts. The study areas are:
- Leicestershire, including the City of Leicester
- City of Manchester
- London Borough of Southwark
- Southampton and the Districts of Eastleigh, Winchester, New Forest and Test Valley

The main fieldwork for the study was conducted in three stages.

Stage one

The first stage consisted of interviews with managers from fifty-two housing associations. Where the association had schemes in more than one of the study areas, separate interviews were carried out in each area. This gave a total of sixty-one interviews. The sample contained a variety of types of associations. The largest number (48 per cent) were providers of general needs housing which have moved into special needs. A further 40 per cent were exclusively involved in special needs accommodation and 12 per cent had moved from this base into providing housing for general needs.

The aims of the first stage were to collect detailed data on scheme types and to gain information about the priorities and concerns of housing association managers. Interviews were carried out between June and September 1990 following a small pilot study in the Portsmouth area. Associations were selected by reference to the Housing Association Returns (HAR/10) submitted annually to the Housing Corporation. The HAR/10 has no specific category for special needs so we included associations which were listed as providing 'hostels' or 'wheelchair units' and checked to ensure that they met the key study criterion of offering extra support. A small number of associations may have been missed if their schemes were listed under different HAR/10 headings or if they only provided self-contained supported housing.

A large proportion of associations (66 per cent) had between one and four schemes in the study areas. There were five associations with over twenty schemes in one of the study areas, which presented some difficulties for data collection. Where the scheme was managed by another agency, the association manager was not always able to provide the detailed information requested. Some respondents who were scheme-based could not respond to the wider policy questions and others, working at the centre, were unable to provide data on all local schemes. The information on schemes in development (ie planned new schemes not yet open) was in some cases incomplete as final decisions had yet to be taken.

These difficulties resulted in a variable response rate to the questions on scheme characteristics. The rate of response ranged from 80 per cent to 100 per cent, with one question on sources of revenue funding for care and support eliciting a lower response. Statistical analysis of the data relating to the 385 schemes in the study was carried out in late 1990.

Stage two

The second stage of the study comprised interviews with representatives of local statutory authorities. The aims of this stage were to find out how these agencies relate to housing associations and how supported housing fits with local policies and priorities. The sample of statutory agency representatives was identified primarily through information gained from the first stage housing associations. The agencies included in this stage were: the regional offices of the Housing Corporation; housing departments; social services departments; district health authorities; the probation service; and the DSS Resettlement Agency. We carried out twenty-two interviews during May and June 1991.

Stage three

The main aim of the third stage of the study was to explore the views and experience of scheme managers and tenants/residents. As with stage two, this was a small-scale survey intended to illuminate the main research findings arising from the scheme data in stage one. The sample was drawn from those schemes which offered long-term accommodation for the six largest groups represented in the study. Schemes which provided greater permanence were selected as we wished to look at the extent to which supported housing promotes and maintains housing rights and standards for long-term tenants. The sample was also composed to reflect the relative proportions of scheme types found in the first stage (for example, shared/self-contained schemes; 24 hour cover/visiting support). Interviews were held with thirty-five residents and all project managers in seventeen schemes. As a way of selecting residents, we requested interviews with the longest-stay and shortest-stay resident in each scheme. These interviews were carried out during the summer of 1991.

Use of the scheme findings

The selection of housing associations by locality means that the study sample is not nationally representative. The study findings reveal trends in the four study areas and demonstrate the extent to which the development of supported housing is influenced by local factors. Appendix 2 shows some of the variation in provision between areas.

How far can we generalise from the findings of the study about national trends in the development of supported housing? Firstly, in reporting the trends in the four study areas, we have drawn attention to particular local influences where they seem to have had a significant effect on the results. Secondly, our sample of 385 schemes includes a tenant population of between 3,000 and 4,000 people. This we estimate at between 5 per cent and 6 per cent of those accommodated in housing association supported housing in England (this figure is estimated because there are no national figures which include self-contained housing). Thirdly, the study went beyond the four study areas in that we interviewed officers of the Housing Corporation at regional and national level and also representatives of various central government departments. We have also made extensive use of national and regional reports and documentation. Information from these sources generally confirms the picture presented by the findings on scheme characteristics and trends in the four study areas.

Notes

1   Housing Corporation, 1991a
2   Housing Corporation, 1974
3   Department of Environment, 1974
4   Department of Environment, 1974
5   Housing Corporation, 1975
6   Housing Corporation, 1975
7   Housing Corporation, 1991b
8   National Federation of Housing Associations, 1991
9   Housing Corporation, 1989a
10 Housing Corporation, 1989b
11 Niner and Maclennan, 1990
12 Cope, 1990

CHAPTER 1

SCHEME CHARACTERISTICS AND TRENDS

IN EXAMINING the way supported housing has evolved to date, the study poses a number of questions. The first set of questions relates to the groups accommodated: which groups have been given priority, and have these priorities changed? how are needs identified? how do housing associations respond to demands from new groups?

The second set relates to types of accommodation: how far have schemes made use of grouped or dispersed properties? are schemes getting larger or smaller? how much is shared and how much self-contained? what is the association between different types and the various groups accommodated?

The third set relates to the support offered to tenants and the way in which schemes are managed and financed: how many schemes have staff sleeping in and is this changing? what proportion are managed by another agency? to what extent have schemes got funding from non-Housing Corporation sources?

This section of the report gives the detailed findings from our study of 385 housing schemes in the four study areas. All the figures and tables relate to the schemes in the study. Where percentages are used, these refer to the responses obtained rather than to the total sample of 385 schemes. The number of non-responses is recorded in each case as 'not stated'. Due to rounding of the percentage figures, they do not always add up to 100 per cent.

The schemes 'in development' are those for which capital funding was secured at the time of interview (mid-1990) but which were not yet open. The term 'in management' refers to existing schemes with tenants. The proportion of schemes in development was about 20 per cent of the total sample.

Scheme residents

The supported housing sector comprises a great diversity of schemes set up to cater for different groups. We asked the housing association respondents to define the resident group for each of the 385 schemes in the study. The definitions ranged from the very broad (for example, single homeless, young people) to the specific (for example, Asian elders, people with sickle cell anaemia). The broader labels often covered a number of smaller groups, such as ex-offenders or people with alcohol problems in single homeless schemes. Some of these schemes actually did cater for a wide range of needs and others were more specific but used a general description to avoid a stigmatising label. By contrast, a number of respondents named the primary group accommodated rather than giving a more general definition. Thus a scheme described as being for people with mental health problems may have some residents who need support for other reasons.

The growth of supported housing since the early 1970s has been accompanied by rapid expansion in the number of groups on the 'special needs' list. The study shows that, in 1990, planned new provision included schemes for fourteen different groups. This contrasts with the eight groups catered for in schemes set up before 1980 (see Table 1). The Housing Corporation's definition of special needs has changed over time, but it has always allowed for the entry of new groups. The most recent version of the Special Needs Procedure Guide [1] mentions twelve groups but adds that the list is not meant to be exhaustive.

The Housing Corporation list no longer includes single homeless people, although special needs funding is still available for single homelessness schemes if they meet the eligibility criteria. We have included these schemes in our list. Our second additional category of 'multiple disability' is included because of the tendency for people who have both learning difficulties and physical disability to be excluded from schemes for both groups.

The proportion of schemes for frail elderly people in our study (3 per cent) is considerably lower than might be expected from the Housing Corporation's figures, which show that 22 per cent of 'hostel' bedspaces are for elderly people. This difference is partly accounted for by the fact that Abbeyfield societies and Almshouses were not included in our study. These two types of association make up 27 per cent of the total number of housing associations in England. Our analysis by schemes rather than bedspaces further reduces the figure, as our figures show that schemes for frail elderly people tend to be associated with large shared schemes. Conversely, the proportion of schemes for disabled people in our study (7 per cent) is higher than indicated by the Corporation's figures or the National Federation of Housing Associations' 1990 shared housing survey.[2] A high proportion of the schemes for disabled people in our study offer self-contained housing.

The new groups for which provision has been planned in the four study areas during the 1980s include people with multiple disabilities, single parents, refugees and people with AIDS/HIV. The demand for supported housing arising from newly identified needs has not been offset by a decline in demand from the more traditional special needs groups. Schemes for single homeless people, for example, make up 23 per cent of the total schemes in the sample and more than 25 per cent of the planned new schemes. Schemes for young people, another of the groups provided for before 1970, make up 19 per cent of the total schemes and almost 18 per cent of the planned new schemes (see Tables 1 and 2). The figures relating to disabled people are 7 per cent of total schemes and just over 5 per cent of planned new schemes, showing a decline. However, this group was one of the most frequently mentioned when housing association managers were asked about their priorities for the future.

The focus of development has shifted over time. In the early 1980s, for example, over 25 per cent of new schemes were for young people, whereas in the late 1980s a similar proportion were for people with learning difficulties. The four groups most closely associated with government community care policy are people with learning difficulties, people with mental health problems, disabled people and frail elderly people. Schemes for these groups make up about 40 per cent of the total schemes in the study. However, they are the four groups most frequently mentioned in terms of future priorities. This suggests that housing associations may be tailoring their plans to fit in with the perceived priorities of local health and social services authorities. The study also

Table 1 - Number of schemes for each needs group

Group	No. of schemes	%
single homeless people	87	23
young people	70	19
learning difficulties	62	16
mental health problems	52	14
physical disability	26	7
alcohol problems	19	5
ex-offenders	15	4
women in refuge	3	3
frail elderly	12	3
single parents	7	2
multiple disability	6	2
drug problems	3	1
AIDS/HIV	3	1
refugees	3	1
Total	**378**	**100**

not stated: 7

Table 2 - Needs group by date of scheme opening

	pre-1960	1960-1969	1970-1979	1980-1985	1986-1990	development
alcohol problems	0	2 (29%)	5 (22%)	0	9 (7%)	3 (4%)
drug problems	0	0	0	2 (2%)	0	1 (1%)
young people	1 (14%)	1 (14%)	2 (9%)	22 (26%)	14 (11%)	14 (18%)
single homeless	3 (43%)	2 (29%)	4 (17%)	13 (15%)	24 (19%)	20 (26%)
mental health	0	1 (14%)	7 (30%)	5 (6%)	19 (15%)	13 (17%)
learning difficulties	0	0	1 (4%)	19 (23%)	32 (26%)	5 (6%)
physical disability	2 (29%)	0	1 (4%)	9 (11%)	10 (8%)	4 (5%)
frail elderly	1 (14%)	0	1 (4%)	4 (5%)	3 (2%)	3 (4%)
women in refuge	0	0	0	4 (5%)	5 (4%)	3 (4%)
single parents	0	0	0	1 (1%)	2 (2%)	4 (5%)
ex-offenders	0	1 (14%)	2 (9%)	4 (5%)	3 (2%)	1 (1%)
refugees	0	0	0	0	1 (1%)	2 (3%)
AIDS/HIV	0	0	0	0	1 (1%)	2 (3%)
multiple disability	0	0	0	1 (1%)	2 (2%)	3 (3%)
Total	**6 100%**	**7 100%**	**23 100%**	**84 100%**	**125 100%**	**78 100%**

not stated: 61

produced examples of schemes for ex-offenders or single homeless people which had shifted towards a mental health focus in order to attract the DSS allowances payable to residents in registered residential homes.

The proportion of schemes accommodating specific ethnic groups was 5 per cent (21 schemes). The establishment of these schemes since the mid-1980s reflects the emergence of black and Asian housing associations (three in the study) and efforts by some other associations to remedy bias and discrimination in their housing provision. The growing demand from refugee groups was also a factor in at least two of the study areas (Southwark and Manchester). Several housing association managers mentioned gaps in provision for particular groups within ethnic minority communities. These groups included elderly Vietnamese people and black people with mental health problems.

More than three-quarters of the schemes in the study catered for both men and women. There was a higher proportion of women-only schemes (14 per cent) than men-only schemes (9 per cent). In one of the study areas (Southwark), 19 per cent of the schemes were specifically for women. These women-only schemes tended to be much newer than the men-only schemes, some of which were old-style large hostels. For some groups (for example, people with learning difficulties or mental health problems), there was a strong presumption in favour of mixed sex provision. For other groups, in particular single homeless people or those with drink problems, there was a lack of consensus about the merits of providing mixed as opposed to separate accommodation for men and women.

Provision for disabled people, other than in purpose-designed schemes for this group, was generally very poor. One-third of the housing associations in the study were unable to offer housing to someone in a wheelchair in any of their supported schemes, and only seven of the sixty housing association managers said that all their schemes were accessible. Several association respondents said they had sought Housing Corporation funding to make their provision more accessible, but these approaches, unless linked to an individual tenant or applicant, had met with little success.

Needs and priorities

When asked how they selected schemes as priorities for funding bids, association respondents referred chiefly to the financial viability of scheme proposals and the perceived strengths of partner agencies. These factors featured more prominently in selecting schemes than a concern to conform to 'special needs' priorities as spelled out in the Housing Corporation's regional policy statements. The influence of particular local voluntary agencies is shown by the wide variation in provision between the four study areas. Manchester has seven of the thirteen women's refuges in the study, Leicester has five of the six schemes for people with multiple disabilities and Southampton has eleven of the nineteen schemes for problem drinkers.

Many associations have put in considerable time and effort to work up scheme proposals which never reached the stage of forming a bid to the Housing Corporation due to lack of guarantees on revenue funding from local statutory agencies (this revenue funding, often referred to as 'topping-up', is required to provide care and support services to tenants). Respondents also gave examples of schemes which had failed for the same reason after getting a capital allocation from the Corporation. Past experience of failed proposals has led many associations to play safe, both by working with large, well-established agencies and by developing relatively cheap and straightforward schemes. Several association respondents said they wanted to develop schemes offering higher care, but that it was usually too difficult to make them 'stack up' financially.

The practice by which the Corporation establishes its priorities varies between areas and gives differing degrees of freedom to local housing associations. The Corporation's 1992/93 regional policy statement for the North West, for example, gives a target for Manchester of 20 per cent of the annual allocation to go to special needs schemes. The policy statements relating to the other three study areas refer to specific priority groups. The London (South) policy statement gives an overall percentage figure for special needs (20 per cent for Southwark) and a figure for each of five named needs groups (for example, mental health 4 per cent). The East Midlands policy statement does not give an overall percentage figure but lists priority groups (for Leicester, frail elderly people and those leaving institutions). The West Region policy statement lists priority groups for each area but in the case of Southampton it gives a formal role in deciding priorities to the local Special Needs Housing Forum. This forum comprises housing associations and local statutory and voluntary agencies.

The Housing Corporation and local authority respondents tended to view the assessment of housing needs in this field as weak and underdeveloped. The Corporation relies primarily on local authority housing departments for an assessment of priorities, although in some areas it is beginning to look to social services departments as well. Neither of these sources was seen by the Corporation respondents as providing adequate information on the housing needs of people requiring extra support. There was evidence from the study that local statutory authorities see priorities largely in terms of plans for closure and replacement of their own residential facilities. Housing departments are inevitably most concerned with the homeless people whom they have a duty to accommodate. Those falling outside this category of statutory homeless tend to be given less attention, especially in more rural areas where total capital allocations are small and 'special needs' may be less evident. The Housing Corporation respondents wanted to see firmer indicators of need against which they could make judgements and develop funding strategies.

Forms of accommodation

'Hostels should be for people who want a communal style of living and whose needs, temporary or permanent, would not be met by other forms of accommodation'
(DoE, 1974).

'Most people, including those with social or physical handicaps or other special needs, will require ordinary housing'
(Housing Corporation, 1978).

Despite the repeated emphasis on ordinary housing, it has been possible for housing associations to get Housing Corporation funding for many different scheme types, ranging from the self-contained flat to the large residential home. Statements from the Corporation in the late 1970s drew a distinction between the large old-style hostels for single homeless people and the small 'caring hostel'. Housing associations were encouraged to develop small-scale provision and to make use of ordinary housing, but the definitions of 'small' and 'ordinary' were left to individual associations.

Nine types of scheme were identified in the study. These are shown in Table 3. Table 4 shows the growing variety of scheme types in supported housing, particularly in schemes set up from 1980 onwards. The use of clustered and dispersed models has steadily increased. These models account for over 40 per cent of the schemes in development in 1990. The model of the small shared house with up to six residents appears to be on the decline in the study areas, but 41 per cent of the schemes in development are large shared schemes for seven or more residents.

Certain groups tend to be associated with particular types of accommodation (Table 5). Disabled people have a very large proportion of the self-contained provision in the study. Single homeless people and frail elderly people, on the other hand, are more likely to be accommodated in large shared schemes. People with mental health problems and those with learning difficulties are the groups most closely linked with the model of the small shared house.

Table 3 - Types of scheme

Type	No of Schemes	per cent
small shared single unit	116	32
small shared cluster units	25	7
small shared dispersed units	13	4
large shared single unit	132	36
large shared cluster units	5	1
self-contained single unit	5	1
self-contained cluster units	49	14
self-contained dispersed units	8	2
mix of shared and self-contained units	10	3
Total	**363**	**100**

not stated: 22

Key: shared schemes - residents share kitchen and/or bathroom/WC
small shared schemes - between two and six residents
large shared schemes - seven or more residents sharing facilities
self-contained schemes - resident has fully private facilities behind
a locked door
cluster schemes - two or more units grouped together or in
close proximity
dispersed schemes - two or more units which are physically separate
but have a common support system.

Table 4 - Scheme type by date of scheme opening

	pre-1960	1960-1969	1970-1979	1980-1985	1986-1990	development
small shared single	0	0	11 (48%)	21 (27%)	43 (36%)	12 (16%)
small shared cluster	0	0	0	5 (6%)	11(9%)	7 (9%)
small shared dispersed	0	0	0	4 (5%)	4 (3%)	4 (5%)
large shared single	5 (71%)	4 (67%)	10 (43%)	29 (37%)	37(31%)	29 (38%)
large shared cluster	1 (14%)	1 (17%)	0	0	0	2(3%)
self-contained single	0	0	0	0	3 (3%)	2 (3%)
self-contained cluster	1 (14%)	1 (17%)	2 (9%)	14 (18%)	12 (10%)	17 (22%)
self-cont dispersed	0	0	0	1 (1%)	6 (5%)	1 (1%)
mix:shared & self-cont	0	0	0	4 (5%)	3(3%)	2 (3%)
Total	**7 100%**	**6 100%**	**2 100%**	**78 100%**	**119 100%**	**76 100%**

not stated: 76

Table 5 - Types of scheme for each group

	small shared single unit	small shared cluster unit	small shared dispersed unit	large shared single unit	large shared cluster unit	self-cont single cluster unit	self-cont dispersed and unit	self cont (100%) unit	mix shared and self-cont	Total shared schemes
	no %	no %	no %	no %	no %	no %	no %	no %	no %	
alcohol problems	6 **35**	1 **5**	1 **5**	7 **41**	1 **5**	0	1 **5**	1 **5**	0	18
drug problems	1 **33**	0	0	2 **68**	0	0	0	0	0	3
young people	25 **37**	7 **10**	3 **4**	23 **34**	1 **2**	1 **2**	3 **4**	1 **2**	3 **4**	67
single homeless	25 **30**	2 **2**	4 **5**	39 **48**	1 **1**	0	8 **10**	1 **1**	2 **2**	82
mental health	24 **46**	3 **6**	3 **6**	11 **21**	0	2 **4**	6 **12**	2 **4**	1 **2**	52
learning difficulty	26 **49**	6 **11**	1 **2**	12 **23**	1 **2**	2 **4**	2 **4**	0	3 **6**	53
physical disability	4 **16**	0	0	3 **12**	0	0	16 **64**	1 **4**	1 **4**	25
frail elderly	0	0	0	7 **58**	1 **8**	0	4 **4**	0	0	12
women in refuge	0	0	0	12 **100**	0	0	0	0	0	12
single parents	1 **14**	1 **14**	1 **14**	3 **43**	0	1 **14**	4 **27**	0	0	7
ex-offenders	1 **7**	0	1 **7**	8 **53**	0	0	0	1 **7**	0	15
refugees	0	0	0	2 **67**	0	0	0	1 **33**	0	3
AIDS/HIV	0	0	0	0	0	0	2 **67**	1 **33**	0	3
multiple disability	1 **17**	3 **50**	0	1 **17**	0	0	1 **17**	0	0	6

Not stated: 29

The study found that in existing schemes, the most common number of residents was 4-6. For schemes in development, the most common number was 7-12 (Figure 3). The figures also show that the proportion of schemes for 13-25 people is increasing, although those for 25+ residents appear to be in decline. There is an overall increase in scheme size. Some of the new large schemes will be using grouped or dispersed housing models, rather than large shared properties. The study found that 16 per cent of all schemes and 21 per cent of those in development used two or more properties (Table 6). Approximately 22 per cent of schemes were in 'new build' and 59 per cent in rehabilitated properties. The rest were in properties leased from local authorities or re-let from a housing association's general stock.

The study sample contained a small number of large and long-established hostels for single homeless people. These were identified by the housing association respondents with very basic standards of accommodation, an institutional environment and lack of opportunity for residents to develop independent living skills. Several associations had already carried out improvements and others were waiting for the necessary finance to replace or re-furbish their hostel. Such improvements usually involve increasing the private space for each resident and enhancing both individual and communal facilities. This often has the effect of reducing the number of places available.

The study did not produce explicit data on the rise in standards of accommodation within the supported housing sector. However, many housing association respondents mentioned the improved standards in their more recent schemes and referred to schemes set up fifteen or even ten years ago as outdated and substandard. These comments related both to the actual accommodation and to the furnishings and equipment. Dissatisfaction with the standards was not confined to large shared schemes, but applied also to some smaller schemes. Most of the 35 tenants interviewed were happy with the general design of their accommodation, the exceptions being residents of large basic grade hostels. Negative comments from the tenants in general centred on the state of decoration and the lack of private space in shared schemes: 'trying to do everything in one room gets on top of you'.

Figure 3 - Size of schemes

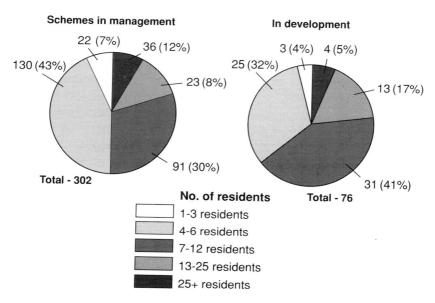

Schemes in management

22 (7%)   36 (12%)

130 (43%)

23 (8%)

91 (30%)

Total - 302

In development

3 (4%)   4 (5%)

25 (32%)

13 (17%)

31 (41%)

Total - 76

No. of residents

☐ 1-3 residents
▧ 4-6 residents
▨ 7-12 residents
▩ 13-25 residents
■ 25+ residents

Table 6 - Number of properties in each scheme

No. of properties	Schemes in management		in development	
single property	250	(84%)	57	(78%)
2-4 properties	30	(10%)	9	(12%)
5-9 properties	8	(3%)	6	(8%)
10+ properties	9	(3%)	1	(1%)
Total	**297**	**100 %**	**73**	**100 %**

not stated: 15

Shared and self-contained provision

*'A self-contained dwelling that is part of the normal
stock ... should always be the first option considered at
the development stage'*
(Housing Corporation, 1978).

The great majority of the schemes in the study (80 per cent) offer some form of shared housing. This is unsurprising, given that the Housing Corporation system of funding for special needs housing has until very recently favoured shared accommodation over self-contained provision. Despite this bias, some of the housing associations in the study have been developing self-contained schemes since the early 1980s and 17 per cent of existing schemes are of this type. The figures for schemes in development show an increase in self-contained schemes to more than a quarter of all planned new schemes (see Table 4). The Special Needs Management Allowance (SNMA) introduced by the Housing Corporation in 1991 is available to both shared and self-contained schemes which meet the eligibility criteria.

The predominant form of accommodation found in the study consists of an individual bedroom with shared kitchen, bathroom and living area. Table 7 shows that almost three-quarters of the schemes (72 per cent) used this model. The proportion of schemes with some shared bedrooms was 7 per cent (26 schemes) and three schemes could only offer accommodation in shared bedrooms. The conversion of shared bedrooms to single rooms was a high priority for several associations, although this presented difficulties by reducing revenue funding. One or two association respondents argued the merits of shared bedrooms as helping the process of integration of a new resident. These were schemes which could be described as having a 'therapeutic' ethos. The other reason given for shared bedrooms was that residents might choose to share with a partner or a friend.

Provision specifically intended for couples was almost non-existent in shared schemes, the assumption being that people would seek to move into independent accommodation. We interviewed one couple living in single bedsit accommodation who are having difficulty finding alternative housing because they are regarded as adequately housed.

Many of the housing association respondents expressed the wish to develop self-contained accommodation, either as move-on housing for their existing schemes or as an alternative to shared provision. The model of self-contained units with additional communal facilities was cited by a number of respondents as particularly appropriate for many people moving from shared accommodation. This model accounts for 6 per cent of the schemes in the study (21 schemes).

The responses of residents to questions about shared living highlight the central and obvious factor of compatibility. If the residents do not get on reasonably well, then the experience of sharing is generally negative. If they do get on together, then it can be very positive and the residents may develop mutually supportive relationships. At its lowest level, a shared scheme requires a certain degree of tolerance between residents if it is to operate successfully. The following quotes are taken from the interviews with residents:

'I wouldn't mix with them under normal circumstances'

'It gets to the stage where you just think 'I need my own space' and become irritable with people'

'I have got used to having people around me...I don't think I could get used to being on my own'

Table 7 - The design of schemes

Facilities	no of schemes	%
single bedroom, shared kitchen and bath	255	72
shared bedrooms	3	1
single bedroom, own kitchen, shared bath	6	2
single bedroom, own bath, shared kitchen	3	1
self-contained, no common facilities	33	9
self-contained, additional common rooms	21	6
mix of single and shared bedrooms	23	6
mix of shared and self-contained facilities	9	3
Total	**353**	**100**

not stated: 32

Shared supported housing cannot be run on the same lines as shared housing in the private sector, where tenants are normally able to exercise a large degree of choice about whom they live with. Housing associations and their partner agencies have a responsibility to respond to housing need and to give priority to those who seem most likely to benefit from the support provided. They also have to be alert to issues of confidentiality and equal opportunities. One manager of a large shared scheme commented that the involvement of residents in selection would lead to the exclusion of the more 'high-risk' residents currently accepted into the scheme. In smaller schemes, it appears to be common practice for potential residents to visit informally to meet existing residents. This also allows the support worker to gain a sense of whether they would fit in with the group.

A number of the tenants interviewed said they had found the experience of moving into shared accommodation very difficult. One said that she felt she had been treated as a scapegoat by the established group of residents and others talked of being 'frightened' or 'terrified' at first. Another respondent said he had found it hard to move back into shared accommodation after his tenancy broke down as he felt that he would be seen as a failure.

Many housing association managers saw shared housing as a stepping stone towards more independent accommodation. There was a strong presumption among housing association managers that most people would prefer self-contained housing. This is borne out by the 1988 study of shared housing residents carried out by the National Federation of Housing Associations, which revealed that 76 per cent of those surveyed wanted their own self-contained flat.[3] Our interviews with project residents showed high levels of satisfaction among those who were living in self-contained accommodation. Among those residents who were sharing, younger people tended to see shared accommodation as a temporary measure and a 'learning experience'. The minority who expressed a wish to remain permanently in shared housing tended to be older people who had previously lived in institutions.

Length of stay

'The Corporation will invest in housing which provides a permanent home for tenants, or equips them with the lifeskills and confidence to move into permanent accommodation'
(Housing Corporation, 1991)

The majority of schemes in the study (60 per cent) provide long-term accommodation (Table 8). We defined long-term schemes as those which offer permanent accommodation or an indefinite (and implicitly long-term) period of stay. At the other end of the scale, 6 per cent of schemes have an expected stay of six months or less and more than a quarter of the total (27 per cent) have a stay of twelve months or less.

Long-term schemes are associated with particular groups, notably frail elderly people, people with learning difficulties, disabled people and those with mental health problems. Long-term schemes represented at least 95 per cent of the provision for each of these groups (Table 9). Short-stay schemes are most strongly associated with women leaving violence, young single parents and young people generally.

Table 8

	Expected Stay	No of Schemes
up to 2 months	3	1
2-6 months	17	5
6-12 months	66	21
1-3 years	40	21
long-term	194	61
Total	**320**	**100**

not stated: 65

Table 9 - Expected stay for different needs groups

Needs group	up to 12 months	1-3 years	long-term	total schemes
alcohol problems	4 (24%)	5 (29%)	8 (47%)	17
young people	30 (50%)	17 (28%)	13 (22%)	60
single homeless	29 (42%)	8 (12%)	32 (46%)	69
mental health	0	1 (2%)	45 (98%)	46
learning difficulty	0	1 (2%)	48 (98%)	49
physical disability	1 (5%)	0	19 (95%)	20
frail elderly	0	0	12(100%)	12
women in refuge	9(100%)	0	0	9
ex-offenders	6 (40%)	4 (27%)	5 (33%)	15
single parents	3 (43%)	3 (43%)	1 (14%)	7
AIDS/HIV	0	0	3 (100%)	3
refugees	1 (33%)	0	2 (67%)	3
multiple disability	0	1 (17%)	5 (83%)	6

not stated: 69

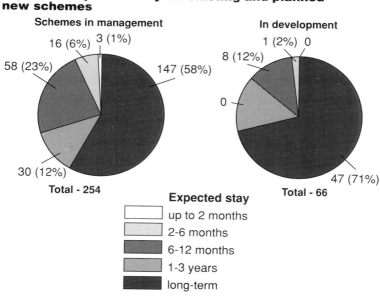

Figure 4 - Expected stay for existing and planned new schemes

Schemes in management

16 (6%) 3 (1%)

58 (23%)

147 (58%)

30 (12%)

Total - 254

In development

1 (2%) 0

8 (12%)

0

47 (71%)

Total - 66

Expected stay

- up to 2 months
- 2-6 months
- 6-12 months
- 1-3 years
- long-term

The study shows a trend in the study areas towards longer-term provision (Figure 4). More than 70 per cent of the schemes in development in 1990 were planned to provide long-term accommodation and under 2 per cent had an expected stay of six months or less. This trend towards long-term schemes can be explained in part by the movement of housing associations towards provision for the four groups most closely identified with care in the community policies (elderly people, disabled people, people with learning difficulties and mental health problems).

The lack of suitable move-on housing and the growth of self-contained provision are prompting more associations to think in terms of permanent accommodation. A high proportion of shorter stay schemes are having difficulties with respect to the availability of move-on housing. Many instances were reported of residents becoming 'stuck' in a transitional scheme for lack of alternative housing. This applied in particular to shorter stay schemes, but respondents also identified the problem of younger and potentially more mobile residents being trapped in schemes which cater for people wishing to stay indefinitely. There was also criticism, both among housing association managers and scheme residents, of the quality of the move-on housing offers made by local authority housing departments. One of the tenants interviewed had accepted the offer of a flat several months previously but could not move in because essential repairs had not been carried out.

The trend towards long-term provision is reinforced by the Housing Corporation's expectation that associations will move towards full tenancy agreements in place of the less secure licence agreement traditionally used in shared schemes. The study could not produce conclusive figures as so many associations were in the process of reviewing their agreements with tenants, but it was clear that the assured tenancy would shortly be the dominant form of agreement. Those who wished to retain licence agreements usually gave as their reason the need for specific clauses (for example, no drinking) and effective sanctions against those breaching these clauses.

More than one in five (21 per cent) of the schemes in the study are registered with social services departments under the Registered Homes Act 1984. The information on the registered homes in the sample shows that more than 78 per cent offer long-term accommodation and a further 9 per cent have a mix of long- and shorter-term stay. This compares with 46 per cent of the non-registered schemes which are long-stay. The association of registered homes with long-stay provision is significant in that residents in these schemes tend to have less security of tenure and in many cases less private space. The study found that one in five of the registered homes had at least some shared bedrooms.

As a counter to the more general trend towards long-stay accommodation, one housing association with a traditionally long-stay shared scheme now prefers to take residents who will 'make progress'. It has introduced a two-year expected stay and is encouraging long-standing residents to move on. One of the residents interviewed said she would prefer to stay in the scheme and that she fears being lonely in her own flat.

Types of support

'The support and care provided by special needs housing schemes is intended to help individuals lead fully independent lives, and to enable them to remain in the community. The main aim of these schemes, however, is to provide appropriate housing'
(Housing Corporation, 1987)

'It minimises the risk of becoming ill again and if I did become ill there would be access to support and help'
'These places do give you that independence with a little bit of back up'
(resident interviews)

The study identified a wide range of support models which we classified into six types. These are shown in Table 10. Visiting support was the most common type, with 38 per cent of the schemes falling into this category. A further 33 per cent of schemes operated with 24 hour staff cover. The groups particularly associated with 24 hour cover are frail elderly people (75 per cent) and people with learning difficulties (74 per cent). Only three schemes involved a system which was negotiated by the tenant as part of an individual 'package' of housing and support. These were schemes for disabled people or people with AIDS/HIV (Table 11). The great majority of the 24 schemes with a warden or supporting tenant used the model of a warden in a neighbouring self-contained property. Associations which had previously provided live-in staff accommodation cited staff dissatisfaction and resident dependence as the main reasons for moving away from this model.

The data for schemes in development indicate a decline in both 24 hour cover and full daytime cover, while visiting support and office hours cover are becoming more common (Figure 5). The lower reliance on intensive staff cover in new schemes suggests that a high proportion of the large shared schemes in development will not be registered as residential homes. Several of the housing association respondents said that they would not develop such provision because of the uncertainty over future revenue support (responsibility for revenue funding will be transferred from the DSS to social services departments in 1993). A small number of associations, particularly those with schemes for frail elderly people, had also experienced great difficulties in obtaining top-up support if their weekly charges exceeded the DSS limits.

The Housing Corporation used to impose a staffing limit on schemes funded through its Housing Association Grant (HAG). The limit was set by a maximum staffing ratio of one staff to two and a half residents. This restriction was abandoned in 1991. The self-contained provision for disabled people offered the best examples within the study of ordinary, integrated housing combined with intensive support.

Table 10 - Range of support

Staff Cover	no. schemes	%
visiting support	135	38
24 hour	116	32
office hours (eg 9am-5pm weekdays)	51	14
warden/supporting tenant	29	8
full daytime (eg 8am-10pm)	19	5
individually tailored to tenant	3	1
Total	**353**	**100**

not stated: 32

Key: *warden/supporting tenant = resident staff member or paid/ unpaid co-tenant or neighbour*
individually tailored = individual housing/support package negotiated by the tenant

The abolition of the maximum staffing ratio might be expected to encourage associations to develop schemes with intensive support. The study showed that for many associations this is an important priority. The demand for high care schemes was found across a range of groups, including young people at risk and ex-offenders as well as people with mental health problems, people with learning difficulties and frail elderly people. In some cases, the demand arose from difficulties in managing existing provision. For example, some of the schemes for young people were having problems due to a change in clientele from young people generally to those needing a great deal of support. This change had generally not been accompanied by an increase in staff and reports were given of a number of such projects which had had to close down either temporarily or permanently. Many associations catering for single homeless or young people also reported an increase in applicants with mental health problems or drug dependency. Respondents wanted to see more provision specifically geared to the needs of these groups.

There have to date been two clear routes to obtaining the revenue support necessary to sustain a relatively high care scheme. The first route involves registration as a residential home and the second the use of staff employed by health or social services authorities. Many of the associations in the study had taken the first route, as indicated by the fact that 21 per cent of the schemes in the sample were registered homes. The proportion of schemes registered ranged from 12 per cent in Manchester to 34 per cent in Southampton and area. There were widely varying attitudes to registration, with some housing association respondents reporting problems to do with institutional design requirements or inflexible rules about staff cover. Some associations indicated that they would not have sought to have schemes registered if there had been alternative ways of securing the finance to meet care costs.

One major problem noted by both residents and managers was the low level of the weekly personal allowance for those living in registered homes and their consequent inability to move away from dependence on the hostel. One resident had given up his part-time job on moving into a registered home as he could only afford the weekly charges by becoming unemployed and relying on DSS benefits.

The second route to providing high care schemes (use of statutory agency staff) had been taken by a number of associations working in partnership with health authorities or social services departments. The schemes concerned were mainly for people with learning difficulties, disabled people and to a lesser extent those with mental health problems. There were about thirty schemes

Table 11 · Types of support for each group

	24 hour cover	full day cover	office hours cover	warden/supporting tenant	visiting support	individually tailored	total schemes 100%
alcohol problems	7 (39%)	1 (6%)	0	1 (6%)	9 (50%)	0	18
drug problems	1 (50%)	0	0	0	1 (50%)	0	2
young people	12 (19%)	4 (6%)	18 (29%)	4 (6%)	25 (40%)	0	63
single homeless	11 (15%)	4 (5%)	10 (14%)	11 (15%)	38 (51%)	0	74
mental health	13 (25%)	4 (8%)	9 (18%)	2 (4%)	23 (45%)	0	51
learning difficulty	42 (74%)	2 (4%)	0	2 (4%)	11 (19%)	0	57
physical disability	6 (24%)	1 (4%)	1 (4%)	5 (20%)	10 (40%)	2 (8%)	25
frail elderly	9 (75%)	1 (8%)	0	2 (17%)	0	0	12
women in refuge	1 (8%)	0	4 (33%)	0	7 (58%)	0	12
single parents	0	1 (14%)	2 (43%)	1 (14%)	2 (29%)	0	7
ex-offenders	8 (53%)	0	4 (27%)	0	3 (20%)	0	15
refugees	1 (50%)	0	1 (50%)	0	0	0	2
AIDS/HIV	0	0	1 (50%)	0	0	1 (50%)	2
multiple disability	4 (67%)	1 (17%)	0	1 (17%)	0	0	6

not stated: 39

33

Figure 5 · Types of support for existing and planned new schemes

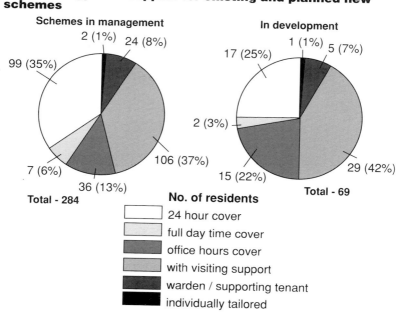

Schemes in management

2 (1%) 24 (8%)

99 (35%)

7 (6%)

36 (13%)

106 (37%)

Total - 284

In development

17 (25%) 1 (1%) 5 (7%)

2 (3%)

15 (22%)

29 (42%)

Total - 69

No. of residents

24 hour cover
full day time cover
office hours cover
with visiting support
warden / supporting tenant
individually tailored

in the study which made use of staff employed by statutory agencies. These schemes have resulted either from a direct agreement between the housing association and the statutory agency or from the setting up of a consortium of local statutory and voluntary agencies. Some of the consortium schemes in the study have employed health authority staff, although the movement is towards direct employment of support workers by the consortium. The study findings did not indicate any general trend towards the establishment of schemes run by housing consortia in the study areas to date (Table 12). However, one area (Manchester) has a newly established housing consortium for mental health and the model was mentioned as a way forward by several statutory agency respondents, in particular those from health authorities.

The NHS and Community Care Act 1990 allows, in principle, for high care to be provided in housing schemes which are not registered as residential homes. It also allows, again in principle, for the development of individual housing and support 'packages' for people wanting to live independently. There was widespread concern among respondents that existing residential home schemes would be threatened when revenue support was transferred from the DSS to local social services departments in April 1993. This concern focused particularly on schemes catering for groups perceived as marginal to the priorities of social services and on those more specialist schemes taking residents from more than one social services area. The lack of any information about how much money would be involved in the transfer and how it would be distributed was affecting the development plans of associations. One respondent commented that 'bids this year will be either low support schemes or schemes where all the staff are provided by the health authority'. The concern over the future of existing residential homes and the belief that funding would prove inadequate had largely blocked consideration of the potential of the 1990 NHS and Community Care Act to encourage more imaginative forms of high support housing.

Management of schemes

The study showed considerable variety in the arrangements for managing schemes (Table 12). We categorised schemes according to the agency which managed the care/support staff. If the housing association employed the support workers, or employed workers with a combined housing management/support role, then we defined the scheme as directly managed.

Almost all the schemes which opened before 1980 were managed directly by the association (Table 13). The trend for schemes to be managed in partnership with a voluntary agency was established in the early 1980s and this trend is still evident for the schemes in development. The development of schemes with statutory agencies also dates back to the early 1980s, although the total number of these schemes is much lower. The proportion of schemes managed in conjunction with a statutory agency ranged from 3 per cent in Southampton to 22 per cent in Manchester. The interviews with health and social services respondents indicated that partnership schemes with these agencies are likely to increase in the future. Several respondents from these agencies referred to the key role that they expect housing associations to play as the statutory authorities seek to provide a 'mixed economy of care' and to replace outdated forms of accommodation.

Table 12 - Types of scheme management

Management model	no. schemes	%
Voluntary agency	170	45
Direct management	157	42
Statutory agency	30	8
Consortium	15	4
Tenant	3	1
Total	**375**	**100**

not stated: 10

Key: Consortium = agencies working together within a legally
        established organisation set up to provide supported housing
        Tenant = care/support managed by individual tenant

The increase in partnership models reflects in part the desire of associations to use the expertise of other agencies in managing more specialised schemes. This has been matched by a growing awareness among other agencies of the advantages, both financial and professional, of working with housing associations. The level of support does not seem to be a factor in the choice of management model, given that directly managed schemes include a higher proportion of registered homes than those managed by partner agencies. For both directly managed and partnership schemes, the study indicated a very high degree of reliance on agency referrals as a filter for the selection of residents. In many cases, responsibility for housing allocation lay with the partner agency, although the association retained the right of veto. The study produced very few examples of schemes where the association operated a waiting list for direct applicants.

Housing associations are not able to delegate management responsibility to a statutory agency as they can with a voluntary agency. The associations in the study differed markedly in their approach to running schemes with statutory agencies. Some would only take on small 'one-off' schemes, while others were prepared to

Table 13 – Management arrangements by date of scheme opening

Date Open	direct management	development for another h assoc	voluntary agency	statutory authority*	consortium	tenant management	total schemes (100%)
pre 1960	7 (100%)	0	0	0	0	0	7
1960 - 1969	6 (86%)	0	1 (14%)	0	0	0	7
1970 - 1979	23 (100%)	0	0	0	0	0	23
1980 - 1985	38 (46%)	0	37 (45%)	6 (7%)	1 (1%)	1 (1%)	83
1986 - 1990	40 (32%)	2 (2%)	59 (47%)	13 (10%)	11 (9%)	0	125
development	25 (32%)	1 (1%)	42 (54%)	7 (9%)	2 (3%)	0	77

* schemes with staffing from a local statutory authority

not stated: 63

consider large-scale developments planned to coincide with the rundown of hospital facilities. The large general needs housing associations were the most likely to be involved in these re-provision programmes. A number of the associations were in the process of setting up new 'care' divisions within their management structure to run residential home and nursing home schemes. Some of these associations were also in discussions with social services with regard to the transfer of the local authority's residential home facilities to housing association management.

Table 14 - Sources of capital funding

Source of capital	No. of schemes	%
Housing Corporation (HC)	262	70
Mixed HC and private finance	8	2
Mixed HC and statutory agency	17	5
Mixed HC and charitable funds	1	0
Local authority (LA)	24	7
Mixed LA and charitable funds	2	1
Dept of Social Security	6	2
Health authority	9	2
Charitable funds	7	2
Leased property	27	7
Private finance	8	2
Other	1	0
Total	**372**	**100**

not stated: 13

The study found one or two associations willing to take on hospital staff in a transfer arrangement with a health authority, although a larger number saw this as too problematic and would only take on schemes where they could employ the new staff directly. The perceived problems in staff transfer related to the dangers of transferring the hospital culture and the widely differing conditions of service in the two organisations. A number of association respondents also commented that the health authority had seen the association's role as simply providing the bricks and mortar. At least one association had lost potential schemes through its refusal to take on existing health authority staff. The impression gained was that many housing associations are still testing the water with regard to developing schemes with statutory agencies. There are few guidelines and associations are establishing very varying agreements with respect to staffing and management arrangements.

Financing of schemes

Most of the schemes in the study (70 per cent) have received all their capital funding from the Housing Corporation (Table 14). The proportion of schemes solely funded by the Corporation has dropped from 85 per cent in the early 1980s to 62 per cent for schemes in development in the four study areas. This reflects both an increase in mixed sources of capital and particular local factors. One of the areas (Southwark) has a high level of funding from the local authority (13 per cent of schemes), largely due to the closure of a large hostel run by the housing department. Another area (Southampton) has an unusually high proportion of its provision in property leased from the local authority (26 per cent). Most of this leased provision is managed by one association. None of the schemes in development involve the use of leased properties. Only ten of the schemes in the sample have had a capital contribution from a charitable source and none of the schemes in development are receiving capital from charities.

There are nine schemes in the study (2 per cent) with full capital funding from a health authority and a further seventeen schemes (5 per cent) with combined capital funding from the Corporation and a statutory agency. These schemes have all opened since the mid-1980s and the majority are registered residential homes. There is a modest trend towards joint capital funding between the Corporation and statutory agencies.

The Housing Corporation has said that it intends 'to look for the capital and revenue costs of (care in the community) schemes to be funded by a transfer of funds from the relevant authorities and departments'.[4] The study found very little evidence that local statutory authorities were planning to increase the amount of capital provided for schemes set up through housing associations. Only one of the social services respondents saw a possibility of using its capital for future housing schemes. Those social services departments with plans for replacement of hostels intended to change the use of hostel buildings rather than to sell them to release funds for housing development. Some health authorities anticipated making capital contributions in the future, but this was generally envisaged as coming through joint finance rather than from mainstream health authority budgets or proceeds from the sale of land or property.

The timing of the study did not allow for an assessment of the effects of the new financial framework for housing associations on special needs development. However, many housing association respondents made reference to the greater complexity of special needs schemes and the higher development risks attached to them. One respondent commented that 'everything about special projects is a problem' and another that the sector was 'almost on the point of chaos'. These remarks were echoed by many other respondents, some of whom doubted their capacity to pursue such developments in the future. The study indicates that specialist housing associations, particularly those engaged in direct management of schemes, felt especially vulnerable. A number of the general needs associations felt there was a question mark over the extent of their future involvement due to the pressures and incentives to 'maximise output' of new homes and to focus on provision for homeless families.

The study identified sources of topping-up finance for care/support services for just over one-third of the schemes in the study. A shortage of revenue is of major concern to many housing associations and voluntary agencies. Topping-up finance tends to be *ad hoc*, negotiated scheme by scheme and often for one year at a time. Some associations were hopeful that the introduction of contracts with social services departments would put the revenue funding on a more secure footing, but there was little to suggest that this was happening during the period of the study. For some associations, there was uncertainty over which statutory agency was the most appropriate or most likely to provide topping-up for new schemes.

The balance of topping-up in fact varied a great deal between the four study areas, with some housing departments, for example, taking a much broader view of their responsibilities than others. In two of the study areas (Southwark and Manchester), housing department and social services respondents said that cuts in grants had led to an extreme shortage of topping-up for housing schemes. This was threatening the viability of some existing schemes. Housing Corporation respondents also expressed their concern over the lack of adequate topping-up by other agencies and its insecure nature.

Summary of Scheme Characteristics and Trends in the Study Areas

Supported housing provision in 1990 included schemes for fourteen named groups. This compares with eight groups catered for in schemes set up before 1980 and five in those set up before 1970.

There is a growing variety of scheme types. Schemes which use clustered or dispersed units/properties account for over 40 per cent of the schemes in development in 1990.

There is a clear trend towards self-contained housing. Self-contained provision accounts for 17 per cent of the total schemes and 26 per cent of the schemes in development.

The model of the small shared house (2-6 residents) seems to be in decline. The most common number of residents in a scheme is 4-6 for all schemes and 7-12 for schemes in development. The proportion of large shared schemes (7+ residents) has increased since the mid-1980s. This type accounts for 41 per cent of the schemes in development.

More than 80 per cent of schemes provide shared housing and 7 per cent have some shared bedrooms. Over 72 per cent of schemes have single bedrooms and shared kitchen, bathroom and living room.

There is a trend towards long-term accommodation. Long-stay schemes account for 60 per cent of all schemes and more than 70 per cent of schemes in development.

More than one in five of the schemes in the study (21 per cent) are registered with social services departments as residential homes. Almost 80 per cent of registered homes provide long-term accommodation.

There has been a decline in 24 hour on-site staffing. Full 24 hour cover applies to 33 per cent of all schemes and 25 per cent of the schemes in development. Visiting support will be provided in 42 per cent of the schemes in development.

Provision developed in partnership with a voluntary agency accounts for 45 per cent of all schemes and 54 per cent of schemes in development. A statutory agency is involved in the management of 8 per cent of all schemes and 9 per cent of schemes in development.

There has been an increase in mixed sources of capital finance, with 62 per cent of the schemes in development in 1990 being solely funded by the Housing Corporation. Just over 2 per cent of the schemes in the study have received full capital from a health authority.

Notes

1 Housing Corporation, 1991
2 National Federation of Housing Associations, 1991
3 National Federation of Housing Associations, 1988
4 Housing Corporation, 1990

CHAPTER 2

INFLUENCES ON SUPPORTED HOUSING

THE ANALYSIS of trends shows that the development of supported housing is not moving in only one direction. There is an increase in self-contained housing but there is also an increase in large shared schemes. There is an emphasis on 'ordinary housing' but there is still a strong association between high care and more institutional forms of accommodation. The proportion of long-term schemes is growing but some associations with long-term shared provision are encouraging residents to move on. This section of the report looks at some of the pressures and influences which have shaped the pattern of provision by encouraging or discouraging particular types of housing and support.

Changing aims and philosophies

The development of alternatives to large institutions has been a central theme in the evolution of supported housing. The 1970s saw an expansion of small-scale shared provision in the form of group homes for people leaving long-stay hospitals. This model emphasised permanence, protection and mutual support. The 'therapeutic community', by contrast, stressed personal growth and change within a highly structured environment. Shared living was fundamental to the philosophy of both models.

The principles of normalisation and 'ordinary living', already implicit in the move to close large long-stay hospitals, began to be articulated in the late 1970s. During the 1980s, there has been increasing emphasis on individual autonomy and independent living. The Housing Corporation expects schemes offering temporary accommodation 'to equip residents with the confidence and skills to move on into permanent accommodation'.[1] The aim of assisting residents to develop or regain lifeskills is central to the support function in a high proportion of schemes. In others, the support is geared to enabling tenants to sustain an independent lifestyle and to make full use of general community services and amenities.

These shifts of focus have led to changes in the way support is provided to tenants. Only a small proportion of shared schemes now have staff living on the premises and a declining number rely on 24-hour cover. The 'family' model of shared living, with a resident housekeeper, is very much on the way out. In many small schemes, the expectations now are that residents will do their own cooking and cleaning. This can be seen as representing a challenge to traditional sex roles, although self-catering in a mixed sex shared scheme leaves the way open to re-assertion of those roles within the resident group. The increase in women-only schemes is due in part to recognition of this problem.

New forms of housing with care/support have been pioneered by disabled people during the 1980s. Consumer organisations such as Centres for Independent Living and coalitions of disabled people have advocated and assisted individuals to set up arrangements which combine independent, integrated housing with personal assistance. This model allows for tenant control and management of the support.

The trends towards long-term and self-contained accommodation reflect the increasing prominence of housing standards and housing rights. Organisations which may previously have viewed accommodation primarily as providing a context for rehabilitation or treatment now put an emphasis on secure, good quality housing. This applies particularly with regard to provision for problem drinkers and drug users. A number of associations working in the alcohol field have developed schemes which use a 'relapse' model or one in which the right to stay in the accommodation is not forfeited by a return to drinking.

The tension between the housing and care elements of a scheme can be seen in other ways. The lack of flexible systems of revenue funding has forced, or at least encouraged the acceptance of high care forms of accommodation which are far removed from 'ordinary' housing. The fragility of topping-up arrangements can present dangers if the residents do not have proper security of tenure. This is illustrated by recent cases in which health authorities have sought to move people out of housing schemes because of the high support costs.

Involvement of health and social services authorities

The closure of long-stay hospitals was given impetus by the government's 1981 'Care in the Community' policy paper. The document put forward proposals for transferring patients and resources to the community. The proposals included the sale of hospital land and buildings to release resources for housing development. The 1983 Health and Social Services and Social Security (Adjudications) Act introduced the Care in the Community initiative, which was specifically aimed at moving people out of long-stay hospitals. This Act gave powers to health authorities to provide capital finance to housing associations for housing linked to hospital closures.

In the early 1980s, 'care in the community' was thus intimately bound up with hospital closure programmes. The rapid growth in housing association schemes for people with learning difficulties and people with mental health problems during the 1980s was largely due to the effects of such closures. Elderly people and disabled people had a much lower profile as hospital facilities for these groups were by and large not targeted for closure. Health authorities were in fact still developing long-stay hospital facilities in the form of Young Disabled Units, a model introduced in the 1970s as a way of keeping younger people out of geriatric wards. This illustrates the strong association of physical disability with medical models of care. Other reasons why disabled people in long-stay hospitals have not been seen as a priority group were that their numbers were relatively small and care costs in the community perceived to be high. The main thrust of care in the community policy was the rundown and closure of psychiatric and mental handicap hospitals.

Health authorities have not always chosen to work with housing associations. Many have developed their own alternative accommodation, usually designed 'in-house' and often located in the grounds of hospitals. There has been no comparative study of these forms of accommodation and those developed by health authorities through housing associations. However, the indications are that the NHS accommodation is likely to contain many institutional features. As one health authority respondent put it: 'our engineers are used to designing hospitals. They go and convert the place as though people are walking round in pyjamas all day'. Where a housing association simply adopts the designs put to it by a health authority, it can perpetuate the same problem. A number of association respondents commented that some health authorities viewed working with housing associations as a means of gaining access to revenue funding in the form of DSS benefits and Hostel Deficit Grant, rather than as a way of ensuring good housing design. There is also the factor of different perspectives. A housing scheme which seems small and ordinary when compared to a hospital ward may appear less so when compared to mainstream housing for single people or families.

Social services departments have turned increasingly to housing associations as their own capital programmes for residential care have slowed down. These programmes produced many new residential homes and hostels in the 1970s. The 24-bed hostel for people with learning difficulties was an example of a new model promoted by policy documents at this time. Large residential institutions perhaps based in old workhouses and accommodating several hundred elderly people were replaced by purpose-built facilities with thirty or forty places. These were often designed on a cluster model comprising several units with six to eight residents in each. Such models are now widely regarded as outdated. There are signs that a new wave of closures involving these types of accommodation will add to the pressures experienced by housing providers in the 1990s.

Health and social services authorities are now moving away from the direct provision of accommodation. The study shows that these agencies expect to rely increasingly on housing associations to meet the housing needs of those who might previously have been accommodated in residential care or hospitals. Their notional plans for alternative housing provision extend to many people needing high levels of support. Attitudes to high care provision are inconsistent. On the one hand, housing associations are seen as offering more appropriate forms of accommodation than that provided by non-housing agencies. On the other hand, there are expectations among some authorities that residential facilities will simply be transferred to housing associations and that high care will thus continue to be provided within residential homes.

Housing Corporation rules and guidance

The Department of the Environment (DoE) has always been concerned to avoid financing schemes which it sees as being the responsibility of other authorities or government departments. In order to qualify for Housing Corporation funding, a scheme has to have a primary purpose to provide housing. This raises the thorny question of when the primary purpose of a scheme shifts from providing housing to providing care.

The initial assumptions in the 1970s were that housing association schemes offered low support. The Corporation's 1977 Caring Hostels circular said schemes could offer a 'moderate' degree of care, as long as the care costs were met by other agencies. At this stage, residential homes registered as 'Part III' accommodation under the National Assistance Act 1948 were specifically excluded. When the 1984 Registered Homes Act was introduced, however, it was recognised that a significant number of housing association schemes would have to be registered with social services departments as residential homes. The Housing Corporation has continued to provide capital finance for new registered home schemes.

The special needs housing sector has developed as a distinct arm of housing association activity and one that is largely separate from the provision of general needs housing. Special needs schemes have required additional revenue funding which the Corporation provided through Hostel Deficit Grant (HDG). The existence of HDG created a category which pulled in otherwise disparate schemes and the rules attached to this funding (for example, a minimum of six residents) had a strong influence on the types of schemes developed. These separate funding arrangements encouraged the tendency to develop supported housing provision in the form of discrete and recognisable 'special projects'. Up until April 1991, the equation of shared housing with special needs was reflected in the funding system, if not always in the statements of the DoE and the Housing Corporation. The combination of the introduction of Special Needs Management Allowance (SNMA) in 1991 and the reduction in capital allowances for shared housing from 1992 may now result in a funding bias towards self-contained housing.

The extension of revenue funding (SNMA) to self-contained housing marks an important departure for the Housing Corporation. Its Special Needs Procedure Guide states that it wishes to invest in housing that is 'as ordinary as possible'. It advocates consultation with residents, saying that: 'decisions to provide shared rather than self-contained housing must always be taken in the context of knowledge of the type of housing the client group need and prefer'.[2] The limitations on type of scheme and levels of care which were inherent in the eligibility criteria for Hostel Deficit Grant have been replaced by cash limits as represented by the ceiling of 3,000 new SNMA-funded places per year. The SNMA rules also exclude any scheme which receives an element of capital funding from another public source, such as a health or social services authority.

The Housing Corporation has played an important role in promoting housing standards. This is highlighted by a number of comments from respondents on the decision by the Department of Social Security to use an alternative agency to the Housing Corporation to manage its replacement programme for DSS resettlement units. This replacement, which involves developing alternatives to basic grade hostel accommodation for many hundreds of single homeless people, is being carried out on a 'nil-cost' basis. The impossibility of 'squaring the circle' of replacing outdated hostels with modern accommodation at no extra cost was mentioned by several housing association respondents.

The Housing Corporation has also paid serious attention to the housing rights of supported housing tenants. The Corporation's 'Tenants Guarantee' for shared housing and hostels puts emphasis on security of tenure, written legal agreements, affordability of the housing and high standards of maintenance. The Tenants' Guarantee is an important step, although it does not represent a set of legal rights which can be enforced by the action of residents.

Housing policy and developments in community care

After the 1974 Housing Act, housing associations were expected to fill the gaps left by the broader sweep of local authority housing. Their role was not to develop and implement broad housing strategies, but rather to provide for neglected groups and those seen as having more complex housing needs. Following the 1977 Housing (Homeless Persons) Act, associations were advised to consider the needs of people not given priority by local councils, some of the suggested groups being 'recovering alcoholics, drug abusers and ex-offenders'.[3] The 'hidden homelessness of mentally ill and mentally handicapped people' living in hospital or with their parents was also highlighted, as was the gap in provision for elderly people needing a level of care lower than that provided in residential homes.

Housing associations were thus strongly identified with housing for groups officially defined as 'non-priority'. As the above list shows, there was overlap between 'special needs' and non-priority homelessness. Special needs has been used both by the housing association movement and by government departments as offering proof and legitimation of the distinctive role of housing associations:

'The housing association movement has really been one long succession of special projects' (NFHA, 1981)

'The case for housing associations stems from their ability to meet special needs' (Housing Corporation, 1985)

The 1987 Housing White Paper summarised the housing association movement as offering 'good quality rented accommodation for those with special needs or on low incomes'.[4] The paradox in recent policy developments is that these features, which are used to justify the elevation of housing associations from their supplementary role, are the very features most likely to be undermined by the provisions of the 1988 Housing Act. A new culture emphasising enterprise, corporate planning and 'value for money' has been superimposed on the traditional culture of housing associations with its focus on housing need, voluntarism and neglected groups.

Now they no longer have a secondary role as providers of

public rented housing, associations are expected to concentrate on meeting the housing needs of those for whom local housing departments have a legal responsibility to find accommodation. This will have an effect on the special needs sector:

'In the current planning period, ministers have requested us to devote a larger share of our resources to providing general family housing - especially for the homeless. This creates pressure on the share of resources devoted to meeting special needs.'[5]

This shift in focus comes at a time of rising demand for supported housing. An increase in demand is indicated by several factors, including: the continuation of hospital closures; the plans to replace outdated local authority hostel provision; the increasing number of homeless mentally ill people; the growing population of frail elderly people living in unsuitable housing; the growth of the independent living movement; and the need to meet new and emerging demands, such as that presented by AIDS/HIV.

The Housing Corporation, in arguing for increased capital and revenue contributions from other authorities for care in the community schemes, states: 'we face much pressure to devote a substantial proportion of our allocation to care in the community projects, housing people whose accommodation costs have until now been met from social services or NHS budgets'.[6] The implications are in fact larger than this. The 1990s version of care in the community has much broader goals than the early 1980s version, which was concerned with moving people out of long-stay hospitals. Current care in the community policy, as expressed in the NHS and Community Care Act 1990, aims 'to enable people to live an independent and dignified life at home, or elsewhere within the community, for as long as they are able and wish to do so'.[7] The 'community care' population now potentially includes all those requiring additional support to remain in the community as well as those leaving residential institutions. The housing needs are more difficult to quantify and the task, if the legislation is properly implemented, much bigger.

Notes

1   Housing Corporation, 1987

2 Housing Corporation, 1991
3 Housing Corporation, 1979
4 Department of the Environment, 1987
5 Housing Corporation, 1990a
6 Housing Corporation, 1990b
7 Department of Health, 1990

CHAPTER 3

FUTURE PROSPECTS

'There is a limit to how many things can be changed year after year. It may be good for the soul but it is hard on the spirit. You cannot work with so much uncertainty. It produces strain on tenants, staff and committees' (housing association respondent)

THE LATE 1980s and early 1990s have seen enormous policy shifts accompanied by multiple changes to the capital and revenue funding systems for supported housing. This section of the report explores the implications of these changes for future development and assesses the opportunities and pitfalls which may lie ahead. It suggests both changes in policy and ways in which current policies might be more fully implemented. It outlines action for the Housing Corporation, for relevant government departments, for local statutory authorities and for housing associations themselves. Associations have often played a proactive role in the past: now, more than ever, they need to act in order to sustain the development of supported housing and influence its future direction.

Types of scheme
There is no single preferred model for supported housing. Many people want self-contained accommodation but others want to share, either temporarily or in the long term. The predominance of shared housing is now being countered by the relatively rapid growth in schemes offering individual self-contained housing. The Corporation's new 'special needs' funding system gives incentives to general needs housing associations to provide ordinary units that are part of new mainstream housing developments. The shift towards new building and away from conversion and rehabilitation of older properties will encourage this trend, particularly where associations are developing large sites. More large associations are likely to adopt a policy of including a proportion of special needs

units in such developments. This will assist those setting up new schemes to provide more integrated, non-specialist housing.

This model of development has its dangers as well as its advantages. There will be financial and other pressures on associations to focus on low support schemes which offer accommodation in dispersed units. These pressures come in part from the new financial regime for general needs housing. Associations are expected to develop homes as rapidly and efficiently as possible. In developing a new site, an association may be reluctant to include elements which could hold up the production process either because of negotiations with funding or management agencies or because of deviation from non-standard house design.

The Corporation's Special Needs Management Allowance (SNMA) was designed to control rapidly rising revenue expenditure which was a feature of the final years of Hostel Deficit Grant (HDG). The Corporation and the DoE also intended to simplify the system by operating SNMA as a flat-rate grant payable per bedspace or individual unit. The combination of the flat rate of SNMA and the inclusion of self-contained provision could result in a concentration on cheaper, low support schemes. This is indicated by the number of existing schemes which are presented with major difficulties in transferring from Hostel Deficit Grant to the new SNMA. Such schemes will in future require additional topping-up from other sources. The DoE and the Corporation will be monitoring the effects of the new system prior to its review in 1993. This monitoring needs to pay close attention to the types of scheme coming forward and the levels of support offered to tenants.

The increase in integrated housing as opposed to distinct 'special needs' schemes occupying their own site may also be at the expense of groups perceived as being high risk or unpopular. In principle, dispersed, integrated housing offers the opportunity to reduce stigma and break down prejudices. However, the competition for severely limited new housing resources may work against the agencies representing the interests of such groups. The current bias towards new building is also likely to reduce their chances of securing funding for more traditional schemes using converted or rehabilitated property.

Most of the self-contained supported housing developed to date has taken the form of grouped rather than dispersed units. One variant of this is the type of scheme which provides self-contained units with additional shared facilities or common living space. The use of this model is likely to be extended as it allows associations to move away from shared provision while recognising the risks of social isolation associated with self-contained accommodation. As an alternative to shared housing, it may well be cost-effective in that the demand for move-on housing is likely to be lower than in much shared provision. The Housing Corporation does provide for additional common facilities in its capital costings and associations should take advantage of this when considering ways of extending self-contained provision.

The eligibility of self-contained schemes for SNMA should lead to a better fit between the purpose of a scheme and its design. The Corporation does not prescribe (or proscribe) particular scheme designs and the onus is on housing associations to get the design right. This may often be a matter of weighing up very different benefits offered by the different scheme types. In treading this path, it is important that associations avoid the twin perils of adopting the currently fashionable model or wheeling out 'blueprint' designs they may have used for years.

The limitations of revenue topping-up and the dictates of particular models of support continue to exert a strong influence on the design of schemes. This influence is most apparent in higher care accommodation, which remains distorted towards large shared schemes despite the prevailing principles of ordinary housing and the evidence that intensive support can be delivered in other ways. Schemes do not become 'ordinary' by virtue of being run by a housing association rather than a health authority or a social services department. Without more flexible funding for high care housing, there is limited scope to do other than imitate, usually on a smaller scale, the residential institutions which that housing has replaced.

Many housing association schemes are registered with social services departments as residential homes. The requirements for registration of a residential home call for design features and staffing levels which may not fit with the purpose of the scheme.

The future proportion of registered homes among housing association schemes will depend on the degree to which registration remains tied to certain levels of revenue funding. If the link is broken when social services departments take over the care funding from the DSS in 1993, this should encourage the development of a wider range of high care housing. Thus associations which would otherwise have fitted in with the demands of registration may take the opportunity to set up more imaginative schemes with flexible systems of support.

The growth in newbuild schemes should offer scope for innovative design as well as providing unwelcome opportunities for large-scale, institutional forms of housing. Housing associations need to be clear about the types of schemes they wish to develop and be prepared to argue for specialised or non-standard designs where these seem appropriate. They also need to recognise that particular accommodation models can very quickly become outdated and to ask themselves two questions: will this still be needed in twenty or thirty years time? if not, could it be adapted to other purposes? These questions are particularly pertinent given that supported housing may be now taking on the last generation of long-stay hospital patients and that younger and older people tend to have different housing aspirations.

There is a group of people who want long-term shared housing. They may not always be here but they are at the moment and for the foreseeable future. The extension of funding to self-contained housing is implicit recognition that people should not be afforded less in terms of housing standards simply because they also need extra support. This change should have been accompanied by an increase in costs allowed by the DoE and the Housing Corporation for shared schemes, rather than the decrease that is now coming into effect. Associations developing long-term shared schemes should be able to offer a high degree of private space and facilities to each tenant.

The argument is not so strong for shorter-stay shared schemes, although tenants may often have to stay much longer than planned because they have nowhere else to go. Many people come into supported housing wanting time to sort out their lives and make decisions about their future. They may see it as a 'stepping stone' or a place to develop and regain independent living skills. There will be a continuing need for this type of scheme, despite the problems created by the extreme shortage of suitable move-on housing. The predicted increase in dispersed, self-contained provision may possibly encourage a greater number of large associations to offer a proportion of their new units as move-on housing.

Some old-style hostels are badly in need of replacement or upgrading to modern standards. Associations managing this provision may be faced with the dilemma of whether to give priority to improving/replacing existing schemes or to new developments. The same dilemma faces those in the regional offices of the Housing Corporation who make the decisions on capital funding. There should be a separate pool of money for upgrading of schemes and the resulting 'new' places should not be included in the SNMA limit of 3,000 bedspaces. There should also be much more scope for associations to adapt existing supported housing schemes so they are accessible to disabled people. The system of providing funds to adapt properties for specific identified individuals represents too narrow an approach and one that fails to recognise the need for accessibility at the time of demand.

Assessment of housing needs

The diversity of the supported housing sector reflects the amount of freedom given to housing associations to decide their own priorities. This in turn stems from the origins of associations, most of which were formed in response to particular needs or in order to experiment with model solutions to specific housing problems. The system of annual bids to the Housing Corporation for capital funding has encouraged a scheme by scheme approach. Although in theory bids have to match the priorities of housing departments, the weakness of housing needs assessment and the lack of local strategies for supported housing have led in practice to each scheme bid containing its own justification of need.

This somewhat *ad hoc* system has some major advantages. It has allowed housing associations to work at a local level with small voluntary agencies and self-help groups. It has also enabled associations to develop some unusual schemes and to cater for groups which are small in terms of numbers but which have a clear housing need. In practice, the system also has disadvantages. It relies heavily on the activism and strength of local groups and restricts the access to housing of those who lack a sponsoring agency. This can lead to a local imbalance in provision, with some groups getting more attention and securing substantially more resources than others. The study found that, for partnership schemes, housing associations choose to work with already well-established agencies which have a reasonably secure financial base. The insecurity of revenue funding makes it difficult for new groups and self-help groups to argue their case and demonstrate the viability of their proposed schemes.

Up to now, the assessment of housing needs in this field has largely centred on the needs arising from the closure of large institutions. Thus a social services or housing department or a health authority may outline a strategy for replacement housing and seek the involvement of local housing agencies in planning and implementing the strategy. The timetable for such closures, and their financial significance for the agency concerned, can lead to other housing needs being ignored or given low priority. The Housing Corporation has traditionally viewed needs in terms of the different groups on the 'special needs' list. A local housing department is expected to state which groups it wants to be given priority in the annual allocation of Corporation funds. This way of categorising needs by 'client groups' is also widely used by health and social services authorities. It is inadequate in a housing context because it says nothing about the housing circumstances of the people concerned.

A housing association has the primary function of meeting housing needs and applicants for mainstream housing have to give detailed information about their housing situation. In the case of special needs housing, allocation can be based on distinctions which exclude people in extreme housing need. Thus someone living in an institution with no closure programme may have a much lower chance of moving out than someone whose housing need is related to such a closure. Any assessment of local housing needs should at the very least identify the sources of demand for supported housing in terms of the varying housing circumstances of the people concerned. This would allow the less obvious or 'hidden' needs to be recognised and considered alongside those which happen to fit in with organisational priorities.

The NHS and Community Care Act 1990 has raised expectations that community care planning will involve more systematic methods of assessing area housing needs than have so far been attempted. This would have to be based on much more refined indicators of housing need than are suggested by client group labels. In principle, such assessment could lead to more rational decisions and a more equitable distribution of the available housing resources. A danger is that it could reinforce the tendency for needs to be defined according to the imperatives of the major organisations and that smaller groups and many individuals in housing need could lose out. It is important for this reason that housing associations retain the capacity to develop 'one-off' schemes and to cater for groups which may be of marginal concern to local statutory agencies. They should also be able to develop provision for identified individuals as this is in line with the principles of consumer choice and independent living given so much prominence in community care policy.

Housing associations will in the future be much more closely tied in with the local statutory agencies, particularly social services as the lead authority for the planning of community care services. The strategic planning of housing provision is at an embryonic stage in many local areas, but it is coming. In some areas, housing associations have joined together to develop common policies and agree priorities for funding bids. This puts them in a relatively strong position to initiate or take part in the formulation of housing strategies. These strategies should be informed by the knowledge of housing demand held by housing providers and voluntary agencies and not just dictated by the level of revenue topping-up likely to be available in the short term.

Housing providers need to be alive to the future sources of housing demand, particularly those which remain officially unacknowledged in all the many policy documents surrounding the NHS and Community Care Act 1990. The policy emphasis on keeping people in their own homes and preventing moves into residential care overlooks or plays down some very significant housing needs: those of people wishing to move out of institutions, many of which may not be scheduled for closure; those of people whose 'own home' is the home of a parent or other caring relative; those of people living in temporary 'special needs' housing and needing long-term support; those who are literally homeless or in basic hostel accommodation for lack of any alternative; and those who wish for social or other reasons to move out of their own home into sheltered or extra care housing.

Financing the support to tenants

Housing associations are widely acknowledged as experts in this field. They are also seen, in contrast to local authorities, as having access to capital resources and thus the potential to develop new schemes and extend existing provision. There are growing expectations among local statutory authorities (health, social services and probation) that housing associations will be major providers of accommodation within a framework which promotes a 'mixed economy of care' and the 'purchaser' and 'enabler' role of the statutory agencies. The motivations are philosophical as well as political. Housing associations are seen as appropriate agencies to provide the types of accommodation to which many policy-makers and planners now aspire.

The range of supported housing schemes developed to date indicates the potential of housing associations to further the policy aims embodied in recent or forthcoming legislation. The NHS and Community Care Act 1990 will have the widest effect in that it covers, potentially at least, a broad range of needs. The Children Act 1989 and the Criminal Justice Act 1991 also have major implications for housing in respect of young people and ex-offenders.

The 'special needs' sector is no longer a collection of 'one-off' schemes, but a major provider of housing and community care services. The rising expectations of local statutory agencies need to be matched by proper funding strategies. The role of housing in meeting the policy aims of non-housing legislation also has to be recognised at central government level. Supported housing crosses boundaries and cannot be neatly boxed as the responsibility of this or that department. It is currently the subject of fierce territorial dispute, but this is different from most territorial disputes in that it is ground that nobody wants to hold. The Department of the Environment (DoE) wants to see more action and more money from the Department of Health (DoH), and in line with this the Housing Corporation 'will increasingly look for the capital and revenue costs of such (care in the community) schemes to be funded by a transfer of funds from the relevant authorities and departments'.[1] The DoH shows little sign of accepting or acknowledging the argument. Its 1990 policy guidance on community care says that 'the general aim of keeping people at home longer will have a number of broad consequences, for instance in relation to housing supply and demand. However, changes are likely to happen slowly at first and there should be time to make the necessary adjustments'.[2] The draft DoE circular on community care indicates that it is now falling in with this perception and awaiting evidence of increased housing demand. This approach is disingenuous in that it fails to acknowledge that demand can be suppressed by false premises and policy assumptions.

Supported housing schemes cannot 'plug in' to a system of assured topping-up funding. Topping-up is piecemeal. It is also arbitrary in so far as local statutory funders have no guidelines by which they can judge an appropriate level of topping-up for a specific scheme. This not only leads to the inadequate funding of schemes, but it also offers no safeguards against payment of excessive amounts. Relevant government departments, notably the Department of Health, should develop policies on topping-up funding in response to the introduction of Special Needs Management Allowance by the Corporation. The Home Office is already considering changes to its existing arrangements in the light of SNMA and criticisms of inadequate and uneven funding.

A rational system of revenue topping-up would include some central funding (for specialist schemes or others with a wide catchment area) and broad guidelines on rates of topping-up for different types of provision. Any such guidelines would need to take into account the variation in scheme types and move away from the association of high support with large shared schemes. The boundaries of topping-up responsibility between the different statutory authorities cannot be prescribed and would have to remain subject to local negotiation. As an important principle, however, the responsibilities of health authorities must go beyond providing financial support to those individuals who move out of long-stay hospitals. The rundown and closure of large hospitals has indirect as well as direct effects on the demand for housing (ie the hospital accommodation is no longer there as a refuge or last resort for those who may have relied on it in the past). There are also many disabled and elderly people stuck in hospital wards which are not part of any closure programme.

The introduction of contracts between social services departments and voluntary and private agencies may lead to more assured and long-term funding of certain schemes. Larger and more well-established agencies may be favoured. More large housing associations may be encouraged to set up 'care' divisions and to employ increasing numbers of care staff to run residential and nursing homes.

The transfer of DSS funding for residential homes in 1993 may have various effects, depending on how criteria for funding are interpreted and how much money is available. The terms of the transfer offer the opportunity to develop more flexible financing which allows support to be provided to people in a variety of settings. There is a danger that these settings will be seen in terms of a dichotomy between residential care and a person's 'own home'. There is also a strong possibility that if the transfer of DSS resources in 1993 does not provide adequate funds, there will be very little change in the accommodation options currently available. Priority is likely to be given to the funding of registered homes for the groups traditionally associated with accommodation run by health and social services departments. Registered homes schemes for other groups, unregistered schemes and individual housing/care arrangements may be at risk. It is very much in the spirit of the NHS and Community Care Act 1990 that the supported housing sector is considered for funding alongside residential care and domiciliary services.

The priority of 'special needs'

The current pressures on housing associations are to 'maximise output' and to give priority to family housing. Following the introduction of the 1988 Housing Act and the requirement on associations to obtain private loan finance, the emphasis is on 'value for money'. The special needs sector could not be integrated into the new financial regime as the revenue costs of schemes would not allow for the repayment of private loans. The special needs sector is therefore now funded on different terms from general needs housing. In general, supported housing schemes are more complicated and involve higher risk. The need to secure topping-up funding leads to the failure of many scheme proposals both before and after bids are approved by the Housing Corporation. People needing more support may find themselves increasingly excluded as associations seek to minimise the risk and maximise the production of new homes.

The DoE and the Housing Corporation want to see increased capital contributions from other public sources. At the same time, the eligibility rules for Special Needs Management Allowance (SNMA) exclude schemes which have received any capital funding from such sources. This seems both short-sighted and illogical. It is illogical in that the DoE and the Corporation recognise that supported housing schemes have extra housing management costs. If there is a housing/care boundary which allows the Housing Corporation to say it will not meet care costs, then there is also a care/housing boundary (ie why should health and social services agencies meet the extra housing management costs?).

There has to date been extremely limited capital funding from public sources other than the Housing Corporation and the Housing Association Grant programmes of local housing departments. There are also scant signs that health and social services departments are gearing up to major (or even minor) capital funding programmes for housing. There has however been a modest trend towards mixed capital funding involving the Corporation and a statutory agency. The DoE should provide incentives rather than disincentives to such developments if it does not want to promote the idea that capital funding is the sole responsibility of the Housing Corporation. It may be that the 'deal' is that the Corporation provides the capital and SNMA, while other agencies develop more assured and reliable systems of topping-up revenue funding. This accords with the Corporation's role as housing provider and the role of other agencies as providers of care/support.

The relatively low priority of 'special needs' for the DoE and the Corporation is demonstrated by official funding projections. The funds allocated to special needs development will not rise in line with the rest of the Corporation's programme, but at a lower rate determined largely by the pre-set limits on Special Needs Management Allowance (ie 3,000 units per year). This rate of growth is justified as being more or less the same as in the last few years. It is not based on any analysis of trends in the demand for supported housing.

The reasons for giving high priority to homeless families are obvious enough, given the steep rise in inadequate temporary accommodation by local authorities and the dramatic decline in their available housing stock. Housing departments have to give priority to those they accept as statutorily homeless, of which some 80 per cent are families with children.[3] However, the definition of statutory homelessness is no more than the drawing of a line in a situation of housing shortage. Many of those given no priority by housing departments are literally homeless or in desperate housing circumstances. It is their family circumstances (ie single or without children) rather than their actual need which determines their position as non-statutory homeless. Some single housing applicants will be defined as in priority need as they are vulnerable on account of age or disability. The discretion inherent in this definition can work in favour of an applicant where the local authority takes a broad view of 'vulnerability'. However, an increasing number are likely to fall through the net if the housing shortage worsens and overall homelessness continues to rise.

The categories of 'homelessness' and 'special needs' cannot be separated as neatly in reality as they have been in some recent Housing Corporation policy statements. Many people requiring extra support are literally or imminently homeless. Others are living in wholly inappropriate accommodation, such as basic grade hostels or hospital wards. These facts are known and widely acknowledged. 'Special needs' housing has lost its relatively cosy niche not because it is actually considered deserving of lower priority, but because the housing association movement has been put under too much pressure. Within the context of the new financial regime for associations, the supported housing sector is now seen as an expensive and awkward appendage.

The problem cannot be resolved by shifting responsibility for supported housing to other departments and authorities. People with support requirements should, like others, be able to rely on housing agencies to meet their housing needs. The Housing Corporation has played a very positive role in promoting ordinary housing and insisting that funded 'special needs' schemes have a primary purpose to provide housing. The Corporation has also emphasised the housing rights of tenants. There is enormous momentum in the system and it is too late to turn back. The Corporation should instead be arguing for a level of resources for 'special needs' which will enable it to meet its commitments.

The term 'special needs' has been useful in identifying and responding to the needs of neglected groups, including those who not long ago would not have been considered candidates for housing at all. It has attracted additional financial resources which have been essential to the viability of housing development for people needing extra care and support. Now, however, the term has probably outlived its usefulness. Supported housing provision is heterogeneous and has few common features. It includes some accommodation which is indistinguishable from that provided by associations for single people generally and some which differs from mainstream housing on almost every count. The evidence from this study is that the distance between the two ends is widening and that there is growing diversity and dissimilarity within the sector.

In the present situation of severe housing shortage, intense competition and pressure to produce the maximum number of houses at the lowest cost, 'special needs' has become more than just a stigmatising label. It is a category which, because of its connotations of something 'extra', can conveniently be down-graded as a priority. Supported housing schemes do very often need high capital subsidy and higher management allowances. Many need additional revenue funding for care and support services. The abandonment of the 'special needs' category and the use of more neutral terminology (for example, higher management allowance instead of special needs management allowance) may help to ensure that such provision is increasingly integrated, not only in terms of physical location, but also in the development of policy and the planning of housing strategies.

New ways of working

The expansion in self-contained supported accommodation offers scope for associations and their partner agencies to move away from a focus on discrete 'schemes' and towards a combined approach which includes both schemes and more individual arrangements in the form of housing/support 'packages'. Recent community care legislation and policy guidance could best be described as ambivalent towards the development of such 'packages'. On the one hand, notions of independent living and consumer choice are central to the spirit of the NHS and Community Care Act 1990. On the other hand, housing is given scant attention as a means of enabling independence and choice. The policy guidance on community care mentions the development of 'domiciliary, day and respite services' as the first key policy objective. Later in the document, a 'move to more suitable accommodation' is placed below 'support for the user in his or her own home' in the order of preference for constructing care package.[4] The opportunities for imaginative higher care housing provision presented by a more flexible funding system could thus be undermined by an inherent bias against housing solutions.

Housing associations could confront this problem by playing a more active and direct role in assessing and responding to expressed housing needs. As things stand, it is likely that the implementation of the NHS and Community Care Act 1990 will lead to greater reliance by housing associations on needs assessment and tenant selection by other agencies, notably social services departments. They could take a more proactive approach by encouraging direct applications for housing from people seeking extra support. This would allow individuals to express their housing need without the filter of an intermediary, non-housing agency. The negotiations for care/support would then follow registration on the housing association's waiting list. This model has already been used successfully by small numbers of disabled people. It accords with the role of housing associations as housing providers. Local housing associations could work together and with social services and housing departments in responding to the housing and care/support needs thus identified.

This approach implies the development of housing advice services which would enable people to make informed choices and assist them in influencing the kinds of housing and support provided. The advent of care management and systems of individual needs assessment call for an extension of advocacy in respect of accommodation and care options. Housing associations and their voluntary agency partners are well-placed to initiate such services, and indeed there are already areas where this has begun to happen. The 'single point of entry' to community care services may seem neat to planners and policy-makers, but it is likely to restrict choice and to hamper creative thinking by emphasising the policies and priorities of a single agency.

Notes

1   Housing Corporation, 1990b
2   Department of Health, 1990
3   Niner and Maclennan, 1990
4   Department of Health, 1990

CHAPTER 4

POLICY CONCLUSIONS

THIS SECTION of the report identifies six key policy objectives and puts forward recommendations based on these objectives. The six objectives are:

1. To ensure that housing associations retain the capacity and incentive to develop and manage supported housing

2. To improve the assessment of need for supported housing and to encourage the development of local housing strategies

3. To establish a financial framework and development policies which allow for a range of scheme types and a mix of high and lower care housing

4. To discourage forms of accommodation which are more akin to residential institutions than to mainstream housing

5. To provide adequate and secure revenue funding for care and support services

6. To sustain improvements in the quality of accommodation offered to tenants of supported housing

Recommendations

1.1 The Housing Corporation has played a vital role in promoting and financing 'special needs' housing. People with support requirements should, like others, be able to rely on housing agencies to meet their housing needs. **The DoE and the Corporation should not accord any lower priority to people with support requirements than to other groups in** housing need. **They should instead argue the case for sufficient resources to enable the Housing Corporation to meet its commitments as a major funder of rented housing.** *(p 64)*

1.2 There is no simple equation between homelessness and housing need. Many people with 'special needs' are literally or imminently homeless and others are in wholly unsuitable accommodation or lacking support services. **Homelessness and 'special needs' should not be presented by the DoE and the Housing Corporation as competing priorities.** *(p 63)*

1.3 The current limit for Special Needs Management Allowance of 3,000 new places per year has been set without reference to trends in demand. Historical precedent does not provide an adequate measure of demand at a time of rapidly changing ideas and expectations. **The Housing Corporation should devise methods of identifying trends in demand through more detailed analysis of scheme bids and recording of failed as well as successful proposals.** *(p 63)*

1.4 Schemes with a capital contribution from another public source are not eligible for Special Needs Management Allowance. This is short-sighted and illogical. **The DoE and the Corporation should provide incentives rather than disincentives for mixed funded schemes.** *(p 62)*

2.1 The weakness of housing needs assessment has resulted in inequitable provision of supported housing between different areas and different groups. There is no framework which allows planners to identify and anticipate sources of demand. **The DoE and the Housing Corporation should initiate pilot studies with the aim of designing models of housing needs assessment which could form the basis of local housing strategies.** *(pp 56-59)*

2.2 Individuals should have the means and the opportunity to express their demand for housing without having to rely on the filter of an intermediary, non-housing agency. **Housing associations should take a more proactive approach in encouraging direct applications from people in need of supported housing and negotiating with other agencies as required for the financing of care and support services.** *(p 65-66)*

2.3 This approach implies the development of housing advice and advocacy services aimed at assisting people to make informed choices. **The design of local housing strategies should include provision for such services, including 'outreach' advice services for neglected groups.** *(p 65-66)*

3.1 Supported housing has become increasingly diverse, both in terms of the groups accommodated and the types of schemes developed. **Housing associations need to have clear policies with regard to the types of schemes they wish to develop and those they consider inappropriate. In particular, they need to consider the circumstances which may call for non-standard house design (for example, self-contained flats with additional shared facilities).** *(pp 52 - 56)*

3.2 There are indications that the new capital and revenue funding system for special needs housing may encourage dispersed self-contained accommodation with relatively low support. **The DoE and the Housing Corporation, in monitoring the effects of the new financial regime, should publish information on the types of schemes approved and the level of care/support offered to tenants.** *(pp 52-56)*

4.1 The constraints of revenue finance and assumptions about the physical form or layout of residential homes have led to the perpetuation of institutional features in a minority of new schemes. **The Housing Corporation should issue specific guidance on scheme designs which are considered inappropriate for Corporation funding and design features which associations should avoid.** *(p 54)*

4.2   The setting up of 'care' divisions by general needs housing associations may reinforce traditional approaches to people with high support needs and emphasise care requirements at the expense of housing rights and accommodation standards. **Housing associations which develop or take over residential and nursing homes should establish clear policies regarding tenancy rights and the standard of accommodation provided for individual tenants.** *(pp 54)*

5.1   Disagreements between government departments over funding responsibilities could seriously undermine the potential of the NHS and Community Care Act 1990 to promote imaginative forms of high care housing. **As a matter of priority, the DoE and the Housing Corporation should co-ordinate discussions with the DoH, the DSS, the Home Office and representatives of the voluntary sector with the aim of securing an equitable system for the future funding of supported housing** *(pp 59-61)*

5.2   Such a funding system can only be developed on the basis of shared responsibility. **The following arrangement should be considered:**

a)   the Housing Corporation agrees to finance extra housing management costs in a wider range of schemes, including those capital-funded by other agencies;

b)   the DoH and other government departments develop a system for financing additional care costs and issue broad guidelines for local agencies on levels and sources of funding for different kinds of schemes;

c)   extra care funding should primarily be administered at a local level but there should be central funding for specialist schemes or those with a wide catchment area;

d)   The DoH makes an annual contribution to the Housing Corporation in recognition of the increased housing demand arising from developments in community care policy. *(p 59-61)*

5.3   The rundown and closure of hospitals has both a direct and an indirect effect on housing demand. **The DoH and local health authorities should recognise that the responsibility of health authorities goes beyond providing financial support to individuals leaving hospital as part of a closure programme.** *(p 61)*

5.4   The decision to register a scheme as a residential home is often influenced by the lack of any alternative means of securing adequate finance to meet care costs. **The DSS, DoH and social services departments should use the opportunity provided by the transfer of DSS funds for residential care to break the link between registration of a housing scheme and high care payments.** *(p 61)*

5.5   The future development of housing provision combining ordinary housing with relatively high support depends crucially on a revenue funding system that is flexible enough to take into account a wide variation in scheme types. It also depends on a level of resources which allows for the expansion of new and imaginative solutions as well as the support of existing schemes. **In planning for the transfer of DSS funding in 1993, the relevant government departments should give consideration to the extra resources that will be needed if individuals who need or wish to move are to have a proper choice between different forms of accommodation and care.** *(p 61)*

6.1   A minority of residents prefer long-term shared housing to self-contained accommodation. Others see shared housing as a stepping-stone from which they will move on into their own accommodation. People living in shared housing should not have to experience reduced housing standards. **The DoE and the Housing Corporation should reverse the recent decision to lower the capital cost allowances for shared schemes.** *(p 55)*

6.2   The improvement and modernisation of existing outdated schemes does not produce new accommodation and may often reduce the number of places available. **The finance for upgrading should be additional to the funds made available for new supported housing and any places created through upgrading should not be counted against the limits currently set for Special Needs Management Allowance.** *(p 56)*

6.3   Provision for disabled people, other than in purpose-designed schemes, is generally poor. The system of providing funds to adapt schemes for specific individuals represents too narrow an approach. **There should be additional Housing Corporation resources to improve the accessibility of existing supported housing schemes and clear directives on access for disabled people in all new provision.** *(p 56)*

APPENDIX 1:
HOUSING CORPORATION
DEFINITION OF SPECIAL NEEDS

(Extract from the Housing Corporation's *Special Needs Procedure Guide*, 1991)

2.1 In this guide the term 'special needs housing' is used to describe housing which caters for tenants with a need for a more supportive and intensive style of housing management than is found in 'ordinary' housing.

2.2 The following is a list of people who may require special needs housing:
- people with a physical disability including degenerative and debilitating illness
- people with learning difficulties
- people with mental health related problems
- people with drug or alcohol related problems
- people leaving penal establishments, referred by the probation service or at risk of offending
- refugees
- people with AIDS or HIV
- young people at risk or leaving care
- vulnerable women with children
- women at risk of domestic violence
- frail elderly people

2.3 The list is not meant to be exhaustive or to imply that people who fit a particular category necessarily require special needs housing and the associated management services. For example, people with a physical disability will often not require additional housing management if provided with appropriately designed accommodation.

2.4 Due to a reluctance to label tenants who have complex needs some schemes may have an identified client group of single homeless people. If such schemes meet the special needs eligibility criteria and house tenants who require intensive and supportive housing management they will qualify for special needs funding.

2.5 A 'scheme' for special needs funding purposes is one or more units of accommodation which may range from purpose-built accommodation to dispersed units within general needs stock. Special needs housing may be provided in self-contained or shared accommodation as determined by the needs and preferences of the client group.

2.6 Many special needs schemes will also cater for the care needs of tenants. Capital and revenue funding is available from the Corporation to meet the 'housing' costs of special needs housing. The cost of providing 'care' to tenants will be met by topping-up funding from another source.

Ref: Housing Corporation, 1991

APPENDIX 2:
COMPARISON BETWEEN THE
FOUR STUDY AREAS

Table A: Distribution of housing associations in the study

Manchester	15
Leicestershire	15
Southampton/W Hants	16
Southwark	15

Table B: Number of housing schemes in each study area

Area	No of Schemes	per cent
Manchester	67	17
Leicestershire	77	20
Southampton/W Hants	106	28
Southwark	135	35
Total	**385**	**100**

Table C: Distribution of schemes for named groups

Group	Manch	Leics	Soton	Southwark
alcohol	3	1	11	4
drugs	2	0	0	1
young people	4	22	12	32
single homeless	20	9	17	41
mental health	9	12	20	11
learning diffs	8	10	16	28
phys disability	3	4	15	4
frail elderly	3	5	3	1
women in refuge	7	2	1	3
single parents	1	3	3	0
ex-offenders	5	4	6	0
refugees	1	0	1	1
AIDS/HIV	1	0	0	2
multi-disability	0	5	0	1
Total	**67**	**77**	**105**	**129**

Not stated: 7

Table D: Mixed and single sex schemes

Area	Mixed		Women only		Men only		Total (100%)
Manchester	44	(66%)	11	(16%)	12	(18%)	67
Leicestershire	61	(80%)	9	(12%)	6	(8%)	76
Southampton/W Hants	90	(85%)	7	(7%)	9	(8%)	106
Southwark	101	(75%)	26	(19%)	8	(6%)	135

Not stated: 1

Table E: Schemes for specific ethnic groups

Area	Ethnic minority		General		Total(100%)
Manchester	2	(3%)	65	(97%)	67
Leicestershire	11	(15%)	64	(85%)	75
Southampton	0		106	(100%)	106
Southwark	8	(6%)	127	(94%)	135

Not stated: 2

Table F: Management arrangements

Area	direct management	voluntary agency	statutory input	other	Total (100%)
Manchester	32 (48%)	18 (27%)	15 (22%)	2 (3%)	67
Leicestershire	35 (46%)	35 (46%)	6 (8%)	0	76
Southampton/W Hants	67 (66%)	30 (30%)	3 (3%)	1 (1%)	101
Southwark	23 (17%)	87 (66%)	21 (16%)	1 (1%)	132

Not stated: 12

Table G - Housing schemes registered as residential homes

Area	registered home	%	unregistered	%	Total (100%)
Manchester	8	12	59	88	67
Leicestershire	16	21	61	79	77
Southampton/W Hants	36	34	70	66	106
Southwark	20	16	108	84	128

Not stated: 7

Table H - Capital funding of housing association schemes

	Manchester	Leicestershire	Southampton /W Hants	Southwark
Housing Corporation (HC)	57 (85%)	56(77%)	53 (52%)	96 (74%)
HC joint funding with private source	1 (1%)	5 (7%)	1 (1%)	0
HC joint funding with statutory source	2 3%	4 (5%)	1 (1%)	11 (8%)
HC joint funding with charitable source	0	0	1 (1%)	0
local authority (LA)	4 (6%)	3 (4%)	0	17 (13%)
LA joint funding with charitable source	0	1 (1%)	0	1 (1%)
health authority	0	4 (5%)	1 (1%)	4 (3%)
charitable	0	0	7 (7%)	0
Dept of Social Security	1 (1%)	0	4 (4%)	1 (1%)
leased property (as form of capital)	0	0	27 (26%)	0
private	2 (3%)	0	6 (6%)	0
other	0	0	1 (1%)	0
Total	67 100%	73 100%	102 100%	130 100%

Not stated: 13

APPENDIX 3:
HOUSING CORPORATION CAPITAL FUNDING 1988-1992

There are nine Housing Corporation regions. These tables refer only to the four HC regions which include the areas in our study. 1991/92 figures are provisional. (Source: Housing Corporation)

Table A: Proportion of rented programme allocated to special needs

Region	1988/89	1989/90	1990/91	1991/92
North West	11.2 %	19.4 %	9.8 %	19.5%
East Midlands	24.5 %	25.4 %	22.0 %	21.9 %
West	22.9 %	22.9 %	13.3 %	15.9 %
London (South)	17.5 %	18.3 %	9.9 %	15.6%

Table B - Allocations to named groups 1989/90

Special needs groups	North West		East Midlands		West		London (South)	
	£k	%	£k	%	£k	%	£k	%
alcohol problems	838	1.2%	0	0.0%	449	0.8%	279	0.2%
drug problems	668	0.9%	0	0.0%	0	0.0%	994	0.8%
frail elderly	5220	7.4%	2214	4.5%	5456	9.7%	5074	3.9%
mental health problems	2371	3.4%	2113	4.3%	2628	4.6%	2682	2.1%
learning difficulties	889	1.3%	3700	7.5%	2088	3.7%	3640	2.8%
ex-offenders	471	0.7%	420	0.8%	212	0.4%	102	0.1%
physical disability	1348	1.9%	3255	6.6%	595	1.1%	4026	3.1%
refugees	0	0.0%	0	0.0%	0	0.0%	1841	1.4%
vulnerable women & babies	864	1.2%	42	1.1%	316	0.6%	1239	1.0%
women's aid projects	0	0.0%	370	0.7%	0	0.0%	1050	0.8%
people with AIDS/HIV	0	0.0%	0	0.0%	0	0.0%	0	0.0%
young people at risk	952	1.4%	0	0.0%	1208	2.1%	2880	2.2%
special needs sub total	**1362**	**19.4%**	**12614**	**25.4%**	**12952**	**22.9%**	**23807**	**18.3%**

Table C: Allocations to named groups 1991/92

Special needs groups	North West		East Midlands		West		London (South)	
	£k	%	£k	%	£k	%	£k	%
alcohol problems	0	0.0%	61	0.1%	187	0.2%	977	0.6%
drug problems	0	0.0%	285	0.3%	92	0.1%	0	0.0%
frail elderly	1167	1.2%	5662	6.6%	1430	1.3%	2857	1.8%
mental health problems	4083	4.4%	4315	5.0%	3975	3.6%	4513	2.8%
learning difficulties	1002	1.1%	1921	2.2%	4529	4.1%	3255	2.0%
ex-offenders	1488	1.6%	364	0.4%	122	0.1%	417	0.3%
physical disability	6167	6.6%	3655	4.2%	5042	4.5%	3993	2.5%
refugees	0	0.0%	743	0.9%	444	0.4%	2193	1.4%
vulnerable women & babies	0	0.0%	0	0.0%	878	0.8%	798	0.5%
women's aid projects	114	0.1%	995	1.2%	0	0.0%	1496	0.9%
people with AIDS/HIV	282	0.3%	140	0.2%	0	0.0%	2383	1.5%
young people at risk	3983	4.3%	806	0.9%	1016	0.9%	2138	1.3%
'special' needs sub total	18286	19.5%	18947	21.9%	17715	15.9%	25020	15.6%

APPENDIX 4:
HOUSING ASSOCIATIONS
IN THE STUDY

Anchor HA
Asra HA
Carr Gomm Society
Cecil Houses
Collingwood HA
Cheshire Foundation HA
Christian Alliance HA
Church HA
Coventry Churches HA
De Montfort HA
Downland HA
East Midlands HA
Enham Village Centre
Family HA (Manchester)
Family HA (Southwark)
Foundation HA
Guideposts HA
Habinteg HA
Hexagon HA
Hyde HA
Leicester Family HA
Leicester HA
Leicester Newarke HA
Leicester Quaker HA
Liberty Housing Co-op
London and Quadrant HA
Manchester and District HA
Manchester Methodist HA
Mosscare HA
NACRO Community Enterprises

New Era HA
New Milton HA
North British HA
Northern Counties HA
Patchwork Community HA
Peterloo HA
Raglan HA
Richmond Fellowship
Rotary Club HA (Southampton)
Salvation Army HA
St Vincent's Family HA
Selcare Trust
South East London Consortium HA (SELCHA)
South East London Baptist Homes
South London Family HA
Stonham HA
Swaythling HA
Turning Point
Ujima HA
Wandle HA
YMCA
YWCA

References

Cope, H (1990) *Housing Associations: policy and practice*, MacMillan

Department of the Environment (DoE) (1974) Circular 170/74, HMSO

Department of the Environment (1987) *Housing: the Government's proposals*, HMSO

Department of Health (DoH) (1990) *Community Care: the next decade and beyond, policy guidance*, HMSO

Housing Corporation (HC) (1974) Annual report

Housing Corporation (1975) Annual report

Housing Corporation (1978) Circular, *Housing for single people*

Housing Corporation (1979) Circular, *Hostels: a guide for housing associations*

Housing Corporation (1985) *Corporate Plan*

Housing Corporation (1987) *Schemework procedure guide*

Housing Corporation (1989a) *Housing associations in 1989*, HAR/10 statistical returns

Housing Corporation (1989b) Annual report

Housing Corporation (1990a) Regional policy statement (North West)

Housing Corporation (1990b) Regional policy statement (West)

Housing Corporation (1991a) *Housing associations in 1990*, HAR/10 statistical returns

Housing Corporation (1991b) *Special Needs Procedure Guide*

National Federation of Housing Associations (NFHA) 1981 *Special projects guide*

National Federation of Housing Associations (1991) *Shared housing survey*, summary findings

Niner, P and Maclennan, D (1990) *Inquiry into British housing: information notes*, Joseph Rowntree Foundation